Knife

1 3 5 7 9 10 8 6 4 2

Jonathan Cape, an imprint of Vintage, is part of the Penguin Random House group of
companies whose addresses can be found at global.penguinrandomhouse.com

First published in the United States by Random House in 2024
First published in Great Britain by Jonathan Cape in 2024

This is a work of non-fiction. Some names and identifying details have been changed.

Grateful acknowledgment is made to Liveright Publishing Corporation for permission to reprint
"i carry your heart with me(i carry it in" from *Complete Poems: 1904–1962* by E. E. Cummings,
edited by George J. Firmage, copyright © 1952, 1980, 1981 by the Trustees for the
E. E. Cummings Trust. Used by permission of Liveright Publishing Corporation.

penguin.co.uk/vintage

Printed and bound in Great Britain by Clays Ltd, Elcograf S.p.A.

Book Design by Caroline Cunningham

The authorised representative in the EEA is Penguin Random House Ireland,
Morrison Chambers, 32 Nassau Street, Dublin D02 YH68

A CIP catalogue record for this book is available from the British Library

HB ISBN 9781787334793
TPB ISBN 9781787334809

Penguin Random House is committed to a sustainable future
for our business, our readers and our planet. This book is made
from Forest Stewardship Council® certified paper.

Knife

MEDITATIONS AFTER AN ATTEMPTED MURDER

Salman Rushdie

JONATHAN CAPE
LONDON

ALSO BY SALMAN RUSHDIE

FICTION

Grimus
Midnight's Children
Shame
The Satanic Verses
Haroun and the Sea of Stories
East, West
The Moor's Last Sigh
The Ground Beneath Her Feet
Fury
Shalimar the Clown
The Enchantress of Florence
Luka and the Fire of Life
Two Years Eight Months and Twenty-Eight Nights
The Golden House
Quichotte
Victory City

NON-FICTION

The Jaguar Smile: A Nicaraguan Journey
Imaginary Homelands: Essays and Criticism 1981–1991
Step Across This Line: Collected Non-Fiction 1992–2002
Languages of Truth: Essays 2003–2020
Joseph Anton: A Memoir

PLAYS

Haroun and the Sea of Stories
(with Tim Supple and David Tushingham)
Midnight's Children
(with Tim Supple and Simon Reade)

SCREENPLAY

Midnight's Children

ANTHOLOGIES

The Vintage Book of Indian Writing, 1947–1997 (co-editor)
Best American Short Stories 2008 (co-editor)

This book is dedicated to the men and women

who saved my life

We are other, no longer what we were

before the calamity of yesterday

—SAMUEL BECKETT

CONTENTS

PART ONE

The Angel of Death

1

Knife

At a quarter to eleven on August 12, 2022, on a sunny Friday morning in upstate New York, I was attacked and almost killed by a young man with a knife just after I came out on stage at the amphitheater in Chautauqua to talk about the importance of keeping writers safe from harm.

I was with Henry Reese, co-creator, along with his wife, Diane Samuels, of the City of Asylum Pittsburgh project, which offers refuge to a number of writers whose safety is at risk in their own countries. This was the story Henry and I were at Chautauqua to tell: the creation in America of safe spaces for writers from elsewhere, and my involvement in that project's beginnings. It was scheduled as part of a week of events at the Chautauqua Institution titled "More Than Shelter: Redefining the American Home."

We never had that conversation. As I was about to discover, on that day the amphitheater was not a safe space for me.

I can still see the moment in slow motion. My eyes follow the running man as he leaps out of the audience and approaches me, I see each step of his headlong run. I watch myself coming to my feet and turning toward him. (I continue to face him. I never turn my back on him. There are no injuries on my back.) I raise my left hand in self-defense. He plunges the knife into it.

After that there are many blows, to my neck, to my chest, to my eye, everywhere. I feel my legs give way, and I fall.

Thursday, August 11, had been my last innocent evening. Henry, Diane, and I had strolled without a care through the grounds of the Institution and had a pleasant dinner at 2 Ames, a restaurant on the corner of the green park area called Bestor Plaza. We reminisced about the talk I'd given eighteen years earlier in Pittsburgh about my part in creating the International Cities of Refuge Network. Henry and Diane were at the talk and were inspired to make Pittsburgh an asylum city, too. They began by funding one small house and sponsoring a Chinese poet, Huang Xiang, who strikingly covered the exterior walls of his new home with a poem in large white-painted Chinese letters. Gradually, Henry and Diane expanded the project until they had a whole street of asylum houses, Sampsonia Way, on the city's North Side. I was happy to be in Chautauqua to celebrate their achievement.

What I didn't know was that my would-be killer was already present on the grounds of the Chautauqua Institution. He had entered using a false ID, his fake name constructed out of the real names of well-known Shia Muslim extremists, and even as we walked to dinner and back again to the guesthouse where we were staying, he, too, was there somewhere, he had been there for a couple of nights, wandering around, sleeping rough, checking out the site of his intended attack, making his plan, unnoticed by any surveillance camera or security guard. We could have run into him at any moment.

I do not want to use his name in this account. My Assailant, my would-be Assassin, the Asinine man who made Assumptions about me, and with whom I had a near-lethal Assignation . . . I have found myself thinking of him, perhaps forgivably, as an Ass. However, for the purposes of this text, I will refer to him more decorously as "the A." What I call him in the privacy of my home is my business.

This "A." didn't bother to inform himself about the man he had decided to kill. By his own admission, he read barely two pages of my writing and watched a couple of YouTube videos of me, and that was all he needed. From this we can deduce that, whatever the attack was about, it wasn't about *The Satanic Verses*.

I will try to understand what it was about in this book.

———

On the morning of August 12, we had an early breakfast with the event's sponsors on the sunny outdoor terrace of the Institution's grand Athenaeum Hotel. I don't like a big breakfast, and limited myself to coffee and a croissant. I met the Haitian poet Sony Ton-Aime, Chautauqua's Michael I. Rudell Director of Literary Arts, who was going to introduce us. There was some bookish small talk about the evils or virtues of ordering or not ordering new titles from Amazon. (I confessed that I sometimes did.) Then we walked through the hotel lobby and across a small piazza into the backstage area of the amphitheater, where Henry introduced me to his nonagenarian mother, which was nice.

Just before we went out on stage, I was handed an envelope containing a check—my speaking fee. I put it in the inside pocket of my jacket, and then it was showtime. Sony, Henry, and I walked out onto the stage.

The amphitheater seats over four thousand people. It wasn't full, but there was a big crowd. We were briefly introduced by Sony, speaking from a podium at stage left. I was seated at stage right. The audience applauded generously. I remember raising a hand to acknowledge the applause. Then, in the corner of my right eye—the last thing my right eye would ever see—I saw the man in black running toward me down the right-hand side of the seating area. Black clothes, black face mask. He was coming in hard and low: a squat missile. I got to my feet and watched him come. I didn't try to run. I was transfixed.

It had been thirty-three and a half years since the Ayatollah Ruhollah Khomeini's notorious death order against me and all those involved in the publication of *The Satanic Verses*, and during those years, I confess, I had sometimes imagined my assassin rising up in some public forum or other and coming for me in just this way. So my first thought when I saw this murderous shape rushing toward me was: *So it's you. Here you are.* It is said that Henry James's last words were "So it has come at last, the distinguished thing." Death was coming at me, too, but it didn't strike me as distinguished. It struck me as anachronistic.

This was my second thought: *Why now? Really? It's been so long. Why now, after all these years?* Surely the world had moved on, and that subject was closed. Yet here, approaching fast, was a sort of time traveler, a murderous ghost from the past.

There was no visible security in the amphitheater that morning—why not? I don't know—so he had a clear run at me. I was just standing there, staring toward him, rooted to the spot like a rabbit-in-the-headlights fool.

Then he reached me.

I never saw the knife, or at least I have no memory of it. I don't know if it was long or short, a broad bowie blade or narrow like a stiletto, bread-knife-serrated or crescent-curved or a street kid's flick knife, or even a common carving knife stolen from his mother's kitchen. I don't care. It was serviceable enough, that invisible weapon, and it did its work.

———

Two nights before I flew to Chautauqua, I had a dream about being attacked by a man with a spear, a gladiator in a Roman amphitheater. There was an audience, roaring for blood. I was rolling about on the ground trying to elude the gladiator's downward thrusts, and screaming. It was not the first time I had had such a dream. On two earlier occasions, as my dream-self rolled frantically around, my actual, sleeping self, also screaming, threw its body—my body—out of bed, and I awoke as I crashed painfully to the bedroom floor.

This time I didn't fall out of bed. My wife, Eliza—the novelist, poet, and photographer Rachel Eliza Griffiths—woke me up just in time. I sat up in bed, shaken by the dream's vividness and violence. It felt like a premonition (even though premonitions are things in which I don't believe). After all, the Chautauqua venue at which I was booked to speak was an amphitheater too.

"I don't want to go," I told Eliza. But people were depending on me—Henry Reese was depending on me, the event had been advertised for some time, tickets had been sold—and I was to be paid generously for showing up. As it happened, we had some big domestic bills to pay; our home's whole air-conditioning system was old, on the edge of breaking down, and needed to be renewed, so the money would be very handy. "I'd better go," I said.

Chautauqua, the town, is named after Lake Chautauqua, on whose shore it stands. "Chautauqua" is a word in the Erie language spoken by the Erie people, but both the people and the language are extinct, so the word's meaning is unclear. It may mean "two moccasins" or it may mean "a bag tied in the middle" or it may mean something else entirely. It may be a description of the shape of the lake, or it may not. There are things that are lost in the past, where we all end up, most of us forgotten.

I first came across the word in 1974, around the time that I finished my first novel. It was in the cult-sensation book of that year, Robert M. Pirsig's *Zen and the Art of Motorcycle Maintenance*. I don't now remember much about *ZAMM*, as it was known—I don't really care about motorcycles or Zen Buddhism either—but I remember liking the strange word, and liking, too, the notion of the meetings, "Chautauquas," at which ideas were debated in an atmosphere of tolerance, openness, and freedom. In the late nineteenth and early twentieth centuries, the "Chautauqua movement" spread across America from the lakeside town, and Theodore Roosevelt called it "the most American thing in America."

I had spoken at Chautauqua once before, almost exactly twelve years earlier, in August 2010. I well remembered the cozy, cloistered atmosphere of the Chautauqua Institution, the neat, clean, tree-lined streets around the amphitheater. (But, to my surprise, this was a different amphitheater. The old one had been demolished and rebuilt in 2017.) Within the walls of the Institution, silver-haired liberal-minded folks gathered in an idyllic community and lived in comfortable wooden homes where it didn't feel necessary to lock the doors. To spend time there felt like a step backward in time, into an earlier, innocent world that may only have existed in dreams.

On that last innocent night, the night of August 11, I stood alone outside the guesthouse and looked at the full moon brightly shining down on the lake. Alone, wrapped in the night, just the moon and I together. In my novel *Victory City* the first kings of the Bisnaga Empire in South India claim descent from the Moon God, associating themselves with the "Lunar Lineage," whose members included Lord Krishna and the mighty Achilles-like warrior Arjuna of the *Mahabharata*. I liked the idea that, instead of mere Earthlings going up to the moon in a ship oddly named after the Greek sun god Apollo, lunar deities had descended from the satellite to Earth. I stood there in the moonlight for a while and let my mind run on moon-stuff. I thought about the apocryphal story of Neil Armstrong setting foot on the moon and muttering, "Good luck, Mr. Gorsky," because as a young boy in Ohio he had heard his neighbors the Gorskys quarreling over Mr. G.'s desire for a blowjob. "When the boy next door walks on the moon, that's when you'll get that," Mrs. Gorsky replied. Sadly, the story was not true, but my friend Allegra Huston had made a funny film about it.

And I thought about "The Distance of the Moon," Italo Calvino's story in *Cosmicomics* about a time when the moon was much closer to the Earth than it is now and lovers could leap up to it for romantic moon-trysts.

And I thought about Tex Avery's cartoon *Billy Boy*, about the little goat that ate the moon.

This is the free-associative way in which my mind works.

Eventually, I also remembered Georges Méliès's fourteen-minute silent film *Le Voyage dans la Lune*, the early-cinema classic from 1902 about the first men to reach the moon, traveling in a bullet-shaped capsule fired from an immensely long cannon, wearing top hats and frock coats, and carrying umbrellas. This is the most famous moment from that film—the moon landing:

I had no idea, as I remembered the image of the spaceship wounding the moon's right eye, of what the next morning had in store for my own right eye.

I'm looking back at that happy man, myself, as he stands there soaked in summer moonlight on that Thursday night in August. He's happy because the scene is beautiful; and because he's in love; and because his novel is finished—he only just did the very last thing, correcting the galleys—and its first readers are excited by it. His life feels good. But we know what he doesn't know. We know that the happy man by the lake is in mortal danger. He has no idea, which makes our fear for him even greater.

This is the literary device known as foreshadowing. One of the most celebrated examples of it is the famous beginning of *One Hundred Years of Solitude*. "Many years later, as he faced the firing squad . . ." When we as readers know what the character can't know, we want to warn them. *Run, Anne Frank, they will discover your hiding place tomorrow.* As I think about that last carefree night, the shadow of the future falls across my memory. But I can't warn myself. Too late for that. I can only tell the story.

Here's a man alone in the dark, ignorant of the danger that's already very close.

Here's a man going to bed. In the morning his life will change. He knows nothing, the poor innocent. He's asleep.

The future rushes at him while he sleeps.

Except, strangely, it's really the past returning, my own past rushing at me, not a dream gladiator but a masked man with a knife, seeking to carry out a death order from three decades ago. In death we are all yesterday's people, trapped forever in the past tense. That was the cage into which the knife wanted to put me.

Not the future. The revenant past, seeking to drag me back in time.

———

Why didn't I fight? Why didn't I run? I just stood there like a piñata and let him smash me. Am I so feeble that I couldn't make the slightest attempt to defend myself? Was I so fatalistic that I was prepared simply to surrender to my murderer?

Why didn't I act? Others, family and friends, have tried to answer the question for me. "You were seventy-five years old at the time. He was twenty-four. You couldn't have fought him." "You were probably in shock even before he reached you." "What were you supposed to do? He could run faster than you, and you weren't armed." And, repeatedly, "Where the hell was the security?"

I don't really know what to think or how to reply. On some days I'm embarrassed, even ashamed, by my failure to try to fight back. On other days I tell myself not to be stupid, what do I imagine I could have done?

This is as close to understanding my inaction as I've been able to get: the targets of violence experience a crisis in their understanding of the real. Children going to school, a congregation in a synagogue, shoppers in a supermarket, a man on the stage of an amphitheater are all, so to speak, inhabiting a stable picture of the world. A school is a place of education. A synagogue is a place of worship. A supermarket is a place to shop. A stage is a performance space. That's the frame in which they see themselves.

Violence smashes that picture. Suddenly they don't know the rules—what to say, how to behave, what choices to make. They no longer know the shape of things. Reality dissolves and is replaced by the incomprehensible. Fear, panic, paralysis take over from rational thought. "Thinking straight" becomes impossible, because in the presence of violence people no longer know what "thinking straight" might be. They—we—become destabilized, even deranged. Our minds no longer know how to work.

On that beautiful morning in that attractive setting, violence came running at me and my reality fell apart. It is perhaps not very surprising that in the few seconds available to me, I didn't know what to do.

———

In the first days after the attack, as I lay in my hospital bed with various parts of my body held together by metal staples, I would proudly say to anyone who would listen, "I never lost consciousness, so I remember everything." It's now clear to me that this wasn't true. It's true that I remained blurrily aware of my surroundings, and didn't completely pass out, but not true that my powers of observation were functioning normally, or anything like it. The confidence of my assertion was probably bolstered by the powerful painkillers I was being given at that time—fentanyl, morphine, you name it. What follows, therefore, is a collage, with bits of my memory pieced together with other eyewitness and news reports.

I felt him hit me very hard on the right side of my jaw. *He's broken it,* I remember thinking. *All my teeth will fall out.*

At first I thought I'd just been hit by someone who really packed a punch. (I learned later that he had been taking boxing lessons.) Now I know there was a knife in that fist. Blood began to pour out of my neck. I became aware, as I fell, of liquid splashing onto my shirt.

A number of things then happened very fast, and I can't be certain of the sequence. There was the deep knife wound in my left hand, which severed all the tendons and most of the nerves. There were at least two more deep stab wounds in my neck— one slash right across it and more on the right side—and another farther up my face, also on the right. If I look at my chest now, I see a line of wounds down the center, two more slashes on the lower right side, and a cut on my upper right thigh. And there's a wound on the left side of my mouth, and there was one along my hairline too.

And there was the knife in the eye. That was the cruelest blow, and it was a deep wound. The blade went in all the way to the optic nerve, which meant there would be no possibility of saving the vision. It was gone.

He was just stabbing wildly, stabbing and slashing, the knife flailing at me as if it had a life of its own, and I was falling backward, away from him, as he attacked; my left shoulder hit the ground hard as I fell.

———

Some members of the crowd—unwilling to abandon their picture of the world and look at what was actually happening— thought the attack might be some kind of performance-art stunt intended to highlight the issues of writer safety we had come to discuss.

Even Henry Reese, sitting in his chair, took a moment to adjust his own reality. Then he saw that the man was "all over" me, and he saw my blood.

What happened next was pure heroism.

Henry says that he acted "instinctively," but I'm not so sure about that. Henry, like me, is in his seventies, and the A. was twenty-four, armed, and bent on murder. Yet Henry rushed across the stage at him and grabbed him. In my view a better way of putting it would be to say, He acted according to his best nature. In character, in other words. His courage is a consequence of who he is.

And then audience members, too, acted according to their best natures. I don't know exactly how many people rushed forward to help, but from my position on the floor I was aware of a heap of bodies struggling to hold down my would-be murderer, even though he was young and strong and held a bloodied knife and was not easily subdued. If it hadn't been for Henry and the audience, I wouldn't be sitting here writing these words.

I didn't see their faces and I don't know their names, but they were the first people to save my life. And so that Chautauqua morning I experienced both the worst and best of human nature, almost simultaneously. This is who we are as a species: We contain within ourselves both the possibility of murdering an old stranger for almost no reason—the capacity in Shakespeare's Iago which Coleridge called "motiveless Malignity"—and we also contain the antidote to that disease—courage, selflessness, the willingness to risk oneself to help that old stranger lying on the ground.

And eventually, I believe, an officer of the law showed up and took my would-be assassin into custody. I knew nothing about that. I had other fish to fry.

A gun can be used from far away. A bullet can fly a long way to form a lethal bridge between the killer and the killed.

A gunshot is action at a distance, but a knife attack is a kind of intimacy, a knife's a close-up weapon, and the crimes it commits are intimate encounters. *Here I am, you bastard,* the knife whispers to its victim. *I've been waiting for you. You see me? I'm right in front of your face, I'm plunging my assassin sharpness into your neck. Feel that? Here's some more, and some more after that. I'm right here. I'm right in front of you.*

According to news reports, the A. had twenty-seven seconds with me. In twenty-seven seconds—if you happen to be in a religious frame of mind—you can recite the Lord's Prayer. Or, eschewing religion, you could read aloud one of Shakespeare's sonnets, the one about the summer's day, perhaps, or my own favorite, number 130, "My mistress' eyes are nothing like the sun." Fourteen lines of iambic pentameter, octave and sestet: that's how long we had together in the only moment of intimacy we will ever share. An intimacy of strangers. That's a phrase I've sometimes used to express the joyful thing that happens in the act of reading, that happy union of the interior lives of author and reader.

There was nothing happy about this union. Or perhaps there was for the A. He had reached his target, after all; his blade was entering his target's body, over and over again, and he had every reason to think he had succeeded in his endeavor and was standing on the stage of history, having become the one who had fulfilled an antique threat.

Yes. I believe he might have been happy during our time of intimacy.

But then he was dragged off me and pinned down. His twenty-seven seconds of fame were over. He was nobody again.

———

I remember lying on the floor watching the pool of my blood spreading outward from my body. *That's a lot of blood,* I thought.

And then I thought: *I'm dying.* It didn't feel dramatic, or particularly awful. It just felt probable. Yes, that was very likely what
was happening. It felt matter-of-fact.

It's rare for anyone to be able to describe a near-death experience. Let me say first what did not happen. There was nothing
supernatural about it. No "tunnel of light." No feeling of rising
out of my body. In fact, I have rarely felt so strongly connected
to my body. My body was dying and it was taking me with it. It
was an intensely physical sensation. Later, when I was out of
danger, I would ask myself, who or what did I think the "me"
was, the self that was in the body but was not the body, the thing
that the philosopher Gilbert Ryle once called "the ghost in the
machine." I have never believed in the immortality of the soul,
and my experience at Chautauqua seemed to confirm that. The
"me," whatever or whoever it was, was certainly on the edge of
death along with the body that contained it. I had sometimes
said, half-humorously, that our sense of a noncorporeal "me" or
"I" might mean that we possessed a *mortal* soul, an entity or
consciousness that ended along with our physical existence. I
now think that maybe that isn't entirely a joke.

As I lay on the floor, I wasn't thinking about any of that. What
occupied my thoughts, and was hard to bear, was the idea that I
would die far away from the people I loved, in the company of
strangers. What I felt most strongly was a profound loneliness. I
would never see Eliza again. I would never see my sons again, or
my sister, or her daughters.

Somebody tell them, I was trying to say. I don't know if anyone
heard me, or understood. My voice sounded far away from me,
croaky, halting, blurry, inexact.

I could see as through a glass darkly. I could hear, indistinctly.
There was a lot of noise. I was aware of a group of people sur-
rounding me, arching over me, all shouting at the same time. A

rackety dome of human beings, enclosing my prone form. A *cloche,* in food-world terminology. As if I were the main course on a platter—served bloody, *saignant*—and they were keeping me warm—keeping, so to speak, the lid on me.

I need to talk about pain, because on this subject my own recollections differ considerably from the memories of those around me, a group which contained at least two doctors who had been in the audience. Members of this group said to journalists that I was *wailing with pain,* that I kept asking, *What's wrong with my hand? It hurts so much!* In my own memory, strangely, there's no record of pain. Maybe shock and bewilderment overpower the mind's perception of agony. I don't know. It's as if a disconnect had appeared between my "outward," in-the-world self, which was wailing, et cetera, and my "inward," within-myself self, which was somehow detached from my senses and was, I now think, close to delirious.

*Red Rum is murder backward.—Red Rum, a horse, won Grand National Steeplechase three times.—'73, '74, '77.—*This is the kind of random nonsense that was cropping up between my ears. But I did hear some of what was being said above my head.

"Cut his clothes off so we can see where the wounds are," somebody shouted.

Oh, I thought, *my nice Ralph Lauren suit.*

Then there were scissors—or maybe a knife, I really have no idea—and my clothes were being torn off me; there were things that people really needed to attend to urgently. There were also things I needed to say.

"My credit cards are in that pocket," I mumbled to whoever might be paying attention. "My house keys are in the other pocket."

I heard a man's voice saying, What does it matter.

Then a second voice, Of course it matters, don't you know who this is.

It was probable that I was dying, so what did it matter, indeed. I didn't expect to need house keys or credit cards.

But now, looking back, hearing my broken voice insist on those things, the things of my normal everyday life, I think that a part of me—some battling part deep within—simply had no plan to die, and fully intended to use those keys and cards again, in the future, on whose existence that inner part of me was insisting with all the will it possessed.

Some part of me whispering, *Live. Live.*

For the record, I got everything back—the cards, the keys, my watch, some cash, all of it. Nothing was stolen. I didn't get back the check that had been in my inside pocket. It was bloodstained, and so the police kept it as evidence. For the same reason, they also held on to my shoes. (People have asked me why I'm so surprised that none of my possessions went astray. Why would anyone want to steal anything in such a terrible moment? I guess I'm sometimes more disenchanted about human nature than these questioners. I'm happy to have my suspicions proved wrong.)

There was a thumb pressing against my neck. It felt like a big thumb. It was pressing against the biggest wound, preventing my lifeblood from pumping out. The owner of the thumb kept introducing himself to anyone who would listen. He was a retired fireman, he said. His name was Mark Perez. Or it might have been Matt Perez. He was the next of the many people who saved my life. But in that moment I didn't think of him as a retired fireman. I thought of him as a thumb.

Somebody—probably a doctor—was saying, *Raise his legs up. We need the blood to flow to his heart.* Then there were arms lifting my legs. I was on the floor with my clothes cut off me and my legs waving in the air. I was, like King Lear, "not in my perfect mind," but I had enough consciousness left to feel . . . humiliated.

In the next months there would be many more such bodily humiliations. In the presence of serious injuries, your body's privacy ceases to exist, you lose autonomy over your physical self, over the vessel in which you sail. You allow this because you have no alternative. You surrender the captaincy of your ship so that it won't sink. You allow people to do what they will with your body—to prod and drain and inject and stitch and inspect your nakedness—so that you can live.

I was hauled onto a stretcher. The stretcher was lifted onto a gurney. Then I was being moved rapidly out of the backstage area into the open air, toward the waiting helicopter. Throughout this process, the thumb called Matt or Mark Perez remained in position, pressing down on the wound in my neck. At the helicopter, however, the thumb and I had to part.

What's your weight.

I was beginning to fade, but I understood that the question was aimed at me. Even in my awful condition, I was embarrassed to answer. In recent years my weight had ballooned out of control. I knew I needed to lose maybe fifty or sixty pounds, but that was a lot, and I hadn't been doing a good job of it. And now I had to tell anyone within earshot the shameful number.

I managed to speak in single syllables. *Two. Four. Zero.*

The helicopter was a small yellow-and-black bumblebee with no doors and a strict maximum weight limit. There was no room on board for the thumb called Mark or Matt Perez. Another thumb, or something else, took its place. I was no longer perceiving anything at all clearly.

We were flying. I knew that. I felt the air beneath us, the movement, the urgent activity all around me. The landing was so soft that I didn't realize we were on the ground again. An impression of people running. I'm guessing an anesthetic mask was put over my nose and mouth. And after that . . . nothing.

———

Four days later, the Chautauqua Institution issued a statement which read, in part: "There will be a substantially increased law enforcement presence throughout the Institution. In addition, there will be extensive security protocols activated, many of which will not be noticeable to visitors and residents. The Institution is working with our professional security consultants and multiple law enforcement agencies on additional security enhancements and risk management considerations." (Ten months later, on June 15, 2023, the promised new security precautions were unveiled to the press.)

Stable door closed, one may think, *after horse bolted.*

However, as the attentive reader will have guessed, I survived. In Machado de Assis's wonderful Brazilian novel *The Posthumous Memoirs of Brás Cubas,* the eponymous hero confides that he is telling his story from beyond the grave. He doesn't explain how, and this is a trick I haven't learned.

So, having survived—and there's much more to say about that—I'm unable to escape my mind's fondness for free association.

Knives. Knives in favorite movies, Polanski's *Knife in the Water,* a fable about violence and infidelity. Knives in favorite books. Philip Pullman's "subtle knife" that can cut openings between worlds and allow the bearer to traverse multiple realities.

And of course the butcher's knife with which the protagonist of Kafka's *The Trial* is killed on the book's last page. "'Like a dog,' he thought. It was as if he wanted the shame of it to outlive him."

And two more personal knives.

First: In 1968, after graduating from Cambridge, I went to stay with my parents in Karachi, Pakistan, while trying to figure out what to do with my life. In those days the relatively new local TV station might run one English-language program a night, usually something like an episode of *Bonanza*. The gentleman who was running Karachi TV then, Aslam Azhar, was a friend of my aunt Baji's (Begum Amina Majeed Malik, a distinguished educator and my mother's older sister). She got me an appointment with him, and I made my pitch. If he was willing to run a little English-language programming, I said, why not occasionally make some original material, instead of all the *Hawaii Five-O* reruns? I proposed a production of Edward Albee's one-act play *The Zoo Story*. "Fifty minutes long," I said, "which is the same length as *Columbo*, so it would fit in the same slot. A cast of only two characters, and the set is nothing more expensive than a park bench. So it would be cheap, too." The pitch worked. I directed and starred in the production. It was a lamentably bad piece of work, and mercifully has not been preserved.

At the climax of the play my character had to impale himself on a knife held by the other character. The knife they gave me was not a prop. The blade didn't collapse into the handle. It was a real, no-nonsense knife with a sharp six-inch blade. "What am I supposed to do with this?" I asked the props manager.

"Act," he replied.

Second: Twenty years ago, the novel that became *Shalimar the Clown* was born out of a single image that I couldn't get out of my mind, the image of a dead man lying on the ground while a second man, his assassin, stood over him holding a bloodied knife. In the beginning that was all I had: the bloody act. It was only later that I understood who the two men were and what their story was. When I think about that now, I'm shaken. I don't usually think of my books as prophecies. I've had some trouble with prophets in my life, and I'm not applying for the job. But it's hard, thinking back to the genesis of that novel, not to see the image as—at the very least—a foreshadowing. The imagination sometimes works in ways that even the imagining mind can fail fully to understand.

And the opening line of *The Satanic Verses* also returned to haunt me. *"To be born again,"* sang *Gibreel Farishta tumbling from the heavens, "first you have to die."*

When *The Satanic Verses* was published, in 1988, I was forty-one years old. It was my fifth published book. On August 12, 2022, I was seventy-five years old and looking forward to the publication of my twenty-first book, *Victory City*. More than three-quarters of my life as a writer has happened since—as I used to say—the excrement hit the ventilation system. People who are curious about my work have much more of it to choose from than they did back then, and I tell such people that maybe they should start with a different book rather than "that" one (as people often referred to *The Satanic Verses*).

For many years I felt obliged to defend the text of "that" novel and also the character of its author. It was fashionable in some literary quarters to describe the book as unreadable, a book in which it is impossible to get past page 15. In such quarters people spoke of a "Page 15 Club." A play about the so-called Rushdie Affair called *Iranian Nights* was produced at the Royal Court Theatre in London, and it contained the recurring refrain "It was a book that was impossible to read." I felt the need to defend the text. In addition, many prominent and non-Muslim people had joined forces with the Islamist attack to say what a bad person I was, John Berger, Germaine Greer, President Jimmy Carter, Roald Dahl, and various British Tory grandees among them. Commentators such as the journalist Richard Littlejohn and the historian Hugh Trevor-Roper said they wouldn't mind at all if I was attacked. (I've outlived Trevor-Roper, but I assume Littlejohn is feeling pretty satisfied now, wherever he is.)

I no longer feel the slightest urge to defend the novel or myself. The essays "In Good Faith" and "Is Nothing Sacred?" and the memoir *Joseph Anton* contain everything I have to say on those subjects. For the rest, I am content to be judged by the books I've written and the life I've lived. Let me say this right up front: I am proud of the work I've done, and that very much includes *The Satanic Verses*. If anyone's looking for remorse, you can stop reading right here. My novels can take care of themselves. One of the benefits of the passage of time is that by now there are many younger readers who can approach *The Satanic Verses* as a plain old novel and not some sort of theological hot potato. Some of them love it, some don't, and that's the ordinary life of a book.

Correction: that purely literary approach had become possible until that August day. One of the annoying aspects of what happened to me in Chautauqua is that, for a while at least, or perhaps forever, it has dragged "that" novel back into the narrative of scandal.

But I have no intention of living in that narrative anymore.

2

Eliza

In my essay collection *Languages of Truth* I wrote about the inspiration for and birth of the PEN America World Voices Festival. To avoid repeating myself, I'll just say that if Norman Mailer hadn't been president of PEN back in 1986—if he hadn't raised a ton of money and invited a glittering array of the world's greatest writers to New York City for that legendary Congress at which Günter Grass and Saul Bellow got angry with each other about poverty in the South Bronx, and John Updike used the little blue mailboxes of America as a metaphor of freedom and his coziness irritated a substantial segment of the audience, and Cynthia Ozick accused the Austrian ex-chancellor Bruno Kreisky (a Jew himself) of anti-Semitism because he had met with Yasser Arafat, and Grace Paley got angry with Norman for putting too few women on the panels, and Nadine Gordimer and Susan Sontag disagreed with Grace because "literature is not an equal opportunity employer"—and if I hadn't been the starstruck new kid on the block, if those wild days at the Essex House hotel on

Central Park South hadn't happened, I might never have had
the notion of launching an international literary festival eighteen
years later, in a city that had international festivals of everything,
but not, until then, of literature. And if I hadn't set about creating that festival with the help of PEN's Mike Roberts and Esther
Allen and many other PEN people, and if it hadn't become the
successful annual literary equivalent of baseball's *Field of Dreams*
("If you build it, they will come") . . . then in all likelihood I
would never have met Eliza. But all that did happen, and so I did
meet her, on May Day 2017, in the green room at the Cooper
Union, before the festival's opening event. Maybe all that happened *so that* we could meet. In which case, I have to admit that
we owe our good fortune to Mr. Norman Mailer.

I had been the chairman of the festival for its first decade, but
then I passed its stewardship into other, excellent hands, starting
with Colm Tóibín. By 2017, my only duty, as the co-founder, was
to introduce the opening event and to bring on stage the first
speakers: the great Syrian poet Adonis (Ali Ahmad Said Esber),
who would read in Arabic, and the person who would read the
English translation of his poems, an African American poet entirely unknown to me, Rachel Eliza Griffiths. I went to greet
Adonis (in French—he has no English) and was rewarded by a
dazzling smile from the woman standing next to him, who shook
my hand and introduced herself as "Eliza."

Reader: that smile was hard to ignore.

She preferred to go by her middle name, she said, because it
was the name her mother had always used. As it happens, I go by
my middle name too, so we had that in common. Nobody has ever
called me "Ahmed" except my mother when she was cross with
me, and then she would use both my names: "Ahmed Salman,
come here at once!" Over the years I had made a mental list of
other well-known middle-name users, James Paul McCartney,

Francis Scott Fitzgerald, Robyn Rihanna Fenty, F. Murray Abraham, Lafayette Ron Hubbard, Joseph Rudyard Kipling, Edward Morgan Forster, Keith Rupert Murdoch, Thomas Sean Connery, Rachel Meghan Markle. Sometimes (perhaps too often) I would unleash this list as a party trick, but something in Eliza's smile warned me not to go down that path.

Don't show off, I told myself.

Smart move.

A little more on the subject of names. I would soon discover that her father and every member of her family, as well as almost all of her old friends, called her Rachel. But she had asked me to call her Eliza, and so I did, and do. In the aftermath of her mother's death in 2014, a seismic event in her life, and the inspiration for her fifth volume of poetry, *Seeing the Body*, she wanted to hold on to her mother's version of herself. And that was "Eliza." That's what her mother had often called her and so it was who she wanted to be, and was in the process of becoming.

Nowadays I'd say the Rachel v. Eliza score is somewhere around 50–50. "Eliza" is rising.

Neither of us was thinking romantic thoughts that evening in the green room. I know she wasn't, and as for me, I had been divorced for almost fifteen years, and it was over a year and a half since I'd been seeing anyone at all. I'd recently had a conversation with my sister Sameen—a year younger than me, or, in her opinion, my "much younger sister"—in which we had both expressed the view that the romantic chapters of our lives might be over. And we were okay with that, we agreed. As for me, I had a good life, two wonderful sons, work I loved, dear friends, a beautiful home, enough money. The bad old days were far behind me. I loved New York. There was nothing wrong with this picture. Nothing missing from it. It didn't need another figure in the landscape, another person—a companion, a lover—to complete it. It was already more than enough.

So I was absolutely not looking for romance. In fact, I was actively, determinedly, not looking for it. And then it came up behind me and whacked me behind the ear and I was powerless to resist.

As the Mandalorian of love would say: *This is the way.*

After the World Voices event, as the audience came out onto Cooper Square beneath the gaze of the statue of Peter Cooper on its plinth, a candlelight vigil in support of Black Lives Matter was taking place. The spirit of young Trayvon Martin, whose murder by George Zimmerman, and Zimmerman's disgraceful subsequent acquittal, had inspired the movement that became BLM, was also in the air. Eliza and I joined the crowd and held a candle together. I asked someone to take a photograph with my iPhone, and I'm happy, now, to have an image of that moment, even though nothing happened there—or, perhaps more accurately, nothing appeared to happen. We held the candle for a while and then went our separate ways.

There was a PEN after-party on the roof of the Standard East Village hotel, just a short walk from the Cooper Union. I met Marlon James and Colum McCann for a drink at the hotel's street-level bar and then thought, *Maybe I'll just go home.* They said they were going up to the party and coaxed me to come, even briefly. I hemmed and hawed a bit and then agreed.

On such coin-toss moments a life can turn. Chance determines our fates at least as profoundly as choice, or those nonexistent notions karma, qismat, "destiny."

When I got up to the party the first person I saw was Eliza, and after that I didn't look at anyone else. Whatever hadn't seemed to happen in the green room and at the vigil had apparently happened after all, when we weren't looking. We fell into easy conversation that was just a little bit flirtatious.

The rooftop party space had an indoor area and an outside terrace, separated by full-length sliding glass doors. It was a warm, bright night, and I suggested we go outside and look at the city's lights. She led the way. Following her, I failed to notice something important—namely, that while one of the sliding doors was open, and she had just gone through it, the other one was shut. Striding forward, seriously distracted by the presence of the brilliant, beautiful woman I'd just met, and as a result not really looking where I was going, believing myself to be stepping through an open space, I hit the glass door hard, and fell dramatically to the floor. It was such a goofy, uncool thing to do. There's a P. G. Wodehouse story called "The Heart of a Goof." That would be a good title for this episode too.

My head was spinning. "Don't pass out," I instructed myself fiercely. "Do not fucking faint."

My glasses had broken and cut into the bridge of my nose, so there was blood streaming down my face. Eliza ran to my side and began mopping the blood off my nose. I could hear voices shouting that I had fallen. It was quite a hubbub. But I didn't pass out. I got to my feet with a little help, and, feeling shaken, said that I thought I'd better get myself a taxi and go home.

Eliza came down in the elevator with me. There was a taxi. I got in.

And then Eliza got in as well.

"And," as I liked to say when we began telling this story to our friends, "we've been together ever since."

I also liked to say, "She literally knocked me out."

I believe this is an example of what, in the parlance of Hollywood romantic comedies, is known as "meeting cute."

———

It's clear that if I hadn't had that violent encounter with the sliding glass door, Eliza would never have gotten into a taxi with me.

(She completely agrees with this statement.) She came with me because she was worried about me and wanted to make sure I was okay.

We got back to my place and started talking. We talked until perhaps 4 A.M. At one point she said she was glad that we could be friends now. I replied, "I've got enough friends. This is something else."

That made an impression. *Oh,* she thought, *he's got enough friends.* She was pleased.

She went home to Brooklyn as the sun was rising. After she left I wrote myself a note. "I think I fell in love with Eliza. I hope this is real."

———

This rom-com scene has some strange similarities to the scene of the attack: the broken glasses, the blood (much less blood, but, still, blood), the fall to the floor in a daze, the people crowding overhead. It's a kind of comic foreshadowing. But the great difference is that this is a happy scene. It's about love.

One of the most important ways in which I have understood what happened to me, and the nature of the story I'm here to tell, is that it's a story in which hatred—the knife as a metaphor of hate—is answered, and finally overcome, by love. Perhaps the sliding glass door is an analogy of the *coup de foudre*, the thunderbolt. A metaphor of love.

———

I have always been interested in writing about happiness, in large part because it's extremely difficult to do. The French writer Henry de Montherlant famously said, *"Le bonheur écrit à l'encre blanche sur des pages blanches."* Happiness writes in white ink on white pages. In other words, you can't make it appear on the page. It's invisible. It doesn't show up. Well, there's a challenge, I thought. I like challenges. I began to write a story titled "White Ink on a White Page." Its protagonist was called Henry, a genuflection toward Montherlant, and also toward the Henry of John Berryman's *Dream Songs*. I wanted my Henry to suffer from happiness the way people suffer from incurable diseases, or stupidity. I thought about Voltaire's *Candide* and I wanted Henry to believe, Candide-fashion, that he lived in the best of all possible worlds. I thought, he can't possibly be a person of color if he's happy in that way. He had to be white.

I wrote this opening paragraph: "Henry White was white and happy. For a long time there was nothing more to say about him. All around him were people with unhappinesses worth talking about, but Henry was contented, and therefore a kind of blank. Nobody knew what to make of him. He had been white and happy since the day he was born. However, he did not think of himself as white, because white was the color of people who didn't think it was important to think about their color, because they were just people; color was for other people to think about, people who weren't just people. Happy was Henry's nature, the nature of a human being whose happiness had never been sabotaged, and who thought himself entitled to its pursuit, as the Declaration had assured him long before he was born. Next to the family mailbox on his New England country lane, a little way down from the dentist's house that boasted a white sign in the front yard reading 'Tooth Acres,' he had put up a wooden post bearing a sign of his own. The sign read, 'Happy Home.'" (Footnote: My aunt Baji lived in a house called Happy Home too, on Deepchand Ojha Road in Karachi, Pakistan, a million years ago.)

I stopped there. Maybe I'll finish the story, maybe I won't. I've thought a lot about Henry, Berryman's Henry as well as mine.

Once in a sycamore I was glad
all at the top, and I sang,

Berryman tells us, in the very first "Dream Song." And later
there's India-Henry too:

and Henry was happy & beside him with excitement.
Beside himself, his possibilities;
salaaming hours of a half-blind morning
while the rainy lepers salaamed back

I wanted to do terrible things to Henry in my *Candide* story:
I wanted his parents to die, his fortune to be lost, his *belle Cuné-*
gonde to leave him and then develop syphilis and lose her teeth.
I wanted him to be half-killed in the Lisbon earthquake, and I
wanted the lepers to rob him and laugh at his distress. I wanted
him to be smashed out of the armor his whiteness had given him
and to look at the world through nonwhite eyes, to become
Henry Nonwhite. If he was still happy after all that and content
to cultivate his garden, then his happiness, maybe all happiness,
was a form of simpleton insanity. A delusion. The world is mon-
strous, so happiness is a lie. Maybe in the end there would be an
ending like Berryman's, a bridge to jump off, and be done.

At least such a crazy happiness might not write white.

I never finished the story. It's still alive in some shadowed corner of my brain.

I stopped work on it, I think, because something very improbable happened to me, thanks to that fortuitous meeting with
Eliza: I became happy. Happiness was my story now, not just my
character's, and it didn't write white at all. It was exhilarating.

I was happy—we were happy—for more than five years. Then
a version of the calamity I wanted to visit upon my Henry got

thrown at me instead. Could our happiness survive such a blow? And if it did, would it be a delusion, a way of turning our gaze away from the monstrosity of the world, which the knife had made so clear? What would it mean to be happy in the aftermath of attempted murder? What would it mean—what might it do to us—to stop being happy?

On August 12, 2022, these questions would have sounded absurd, if I'd thought of them. That day, it didn't seem as if anything of me would survive at all.

————

She was beautiful, but her relationship with beauty, she said, was complicated. She loved Rilke, who thought that "beauty is nothing but the beginning of terror that we are still able to bear, and we revere it so, because it calmly disdains to destroy us."

She was made of beauty and terror, equal parts of each. I ordered all her books of poems and read them and understood that her gift, her nature, her being in the world, was exceptional. She wrote:

> *I am an outlaw woman*
> *Shadow-dancing. My life too quick to bruise. What is*
> *The name for those who collect the beautiful.*

I felt like Ali Baba learning the magic words that opened a treasure cave—*Open, Sesame*—and there, its light dazzling the eye, was the treasure, and it was her.

It was my good fortune that she also thought well of me. Years later, her father asked her how we fell in love and she said that soon after we met we were having dinner together in a restaurant and she found herself thinking that all she wanted was to spend the rest of her life with this man. So we each received and gave love. The sweetest exchange of gifts.

Things moved quickly. Our lives *too quick to bruise*. It was only a few weeks until we were living together, even though both of us were, in fact, bruised. (Speaking only for myself, I wore the battle scars of my own checkered romantic past.) Our friends offered words of caution. Hers, who had read unkind and untrue words spoken about me in the media, warned her against me. Mine, who had seen how deeply and often I'd been hurt in the past, asked anxiously, *Are you sure?* This is perhaps the inevitable way of the world when the love being born is not first love, not young love, not innocent, but following upon hard experience. *Be careful,* the world admonishes us. *Don't get hurt again.*

But we went on, boats against the current. Something very strong had come into our lives and we both knew it. As time passed and she met my friends and I met hers, the caveats stopped being issued. Perhaps six weeks after my argument with the glass door, we went for Chinese food downtown, in Tribeca, with the woman who was her dearest friend, the poet Kamilah Aisha Moon, author of two highly regarded volumes of poetry, *Starshine & Clay* and *She Has a Name*. Aisha, another middle-name user, was older and sadder than Eliza (and called her Rachel), but the two were as close as sisters. She and I hit it off pretty well, and the evening was enjoyable and full of laughter. Then Eliza went to the restroom and Aisha immediately leaned forward to look me in the eyes and said with immense seriousness, "You'd better treat her right."

———

The world of poets, I began to discover, was a good deal more intimate than the world of novelists. Poets all seemed to know one another, read one another, hang out together, do readings and events together constantly. Poets called one another on the phone late at night and gossiped into the small hours. To a novelist sitting alone in a room for years and only occasionally popping his head above the parapet, poets looked astonishingly gregarious, like an extended family, like a community. And within the larger poetry community, the circle of Black poets felt even tighter and more mutually supportive. How much they knew about one another! How engaged with one another's work they were, how entwined their lives were! Obviously, there was less money in poetry than in prose (unless you were Maya Angelou, Amanda Gorman, or Rupi Kaur), and it felt as if the economic "smallness" of that world bred deeper human connections. That felt enviable.

The journey across the frontier from Poetryland into Proseville often seemed to go through Memoiristan. Memoirs in this literary moment have become a major art form, allowing our perceptions of the present to be remade through the personal life experiences, the extraordinary pasts, of memoirists. (Just one recent example might be Safiya Sinclair's *How to Say Babylon*, a powerful, richly written memoir of growing up in Jamaica and needing to break away from a tyrannical Rastafarian father.)

Eliza was different. She had always wanted to be a novelist, she told me; when she began to dream of being a writer, that had been her dream. She had written fiction all her life, even before she began to write poetry, in fact; but now, with five books of poetry to her name—four published when we met, the fifth, *Seeing the Body*, on the way—it was time for the novelist to step forward.

I quickly learned that she was held in high esteem by her fellow poets. However, I also half-believed the conventional wisdom that not many poets successfully cross over into the world of the novel. (I knew as an absolute fact that very, very few novelists can cross over into the poetry world. I have published one poem in my life and there's no need to say any more about that.)

So when Eliza told me that she had completed a first draft of a debut novel, I was—let's say—nervous.

She, too, was nervous, and for a time unwilling to let me read the draft. We both knew it was close to impossible for two writers to be together unless they liked each other's work—and by "liked" I mean "really liked, even loved." But in the end she did give it to me, and, to my great relief, I could truthfully say I was impressed. Soon after that, I learned that she was also an exceptional photographer and a great dancer, her crab cakes were the stuff of legend, and she could sing. Nobody has ever wanted to hear me sing or watch me dance, or to eat my crab cakes. As a person who can only do one thing, I was in awe of her multiple talents. It became clear to me that this was not just a relationship of equals—rather, it was one in which I was by some distance the less equal party. Even better than that: it was a relationship not of competitiveness but of total mutual support.

Happiness.

———

There is a kind of deep happiness that prefers privacy, that flourishes out of the public eye, that does not require the validation of being known about: a happiness that is for the happy people alone, that is, just by itself, *enough*. I was sick of having my private life dissected and judged by strangers, tired of the malice of wagging tongues. Eliza was and is a very private person, whose main worry about being with me was that she might have to surrender that privacy and be bathed in the acid light of publicity. I had lived too long in that shadowless brightness, and I didn't want it for her either. I didn't want it for myself.

Something strange has happened to the idea of privacy in our surreal time. Instead of being cherished, it appears to have become, for many people in the West, especially young people, a valueless quality—actually undesirable. If a thing is not made public, it doesn't really exist. Your dog, your wedding, your beach, your baby, your dinner, the interesting meme you recently saw—these things need, on a daily basis, to be shared.

In India, privacy is a luxury of the rich. The poor, living in small, overcrowded spaces, are never alone. Many impoverished Indians have to perform the most private of acts, their natural bodily functions, out of doors. To have a room of one's own, one must have money. (I don't think Virginia Woolf ever went to India, but her dictum stands, even there, even for men.)

Scarcity creates demand, and in the poor majority of the world, a room of one's own—especially for women—is still a thing to be yearned for. But in the greedy West, where *attention* has become the thing most hungered for, where the quest for *followers* and *likes* is the new gluttony, privacy has become unnecessary, unwanted, even absurd.

Eliza and I decided to be private people.

This did not mean we kept our relationship secret. My family knew, and so did hers. Her friends knew, and so did mine. We dined out together, went to the theater, cheered at Yankees games at the Stadium, walked around art galleries, bopped at rock concerts. We led, in short, the ordinary life of New Yorkers. But we stayed off social media. I didn't "like" her, she didn't "like" me. And as a result, for five years, three months, and eleven days, we flew almost completely under the radar.

We showed, I think, that even in this attention-addicted time, it was still possible for two people to lead, pretty openly, a happily private life.

Then, cutting that life apart, came the knife.

When I was twenty years old and at King's College, Cambridge, the eminent anthropologist Edmund Leach was the college provost ("provost" being King's-speak for "president"). That year, 1967, the year of the legendary Summer of Love, of be-ins and Haight-Ashbury and flowers in the hair, Leach delivered the BBC's prestigious Reith Lectures on the radio. They became notorious for one sentence. This was it: "The family, with its narrow privacy and tawdry secrets, is the source of all our discontents."

Nineteen sixty-seven wasn't a good year for the idea of the family, as a young generation—my generation—either turned on, tuned in, and dropped out, as Timothy Leary recommended, or, in America if not in Britain, got drafted and shipped out to Vietnam to the tune of Country Joe and the Fish's "I-Feel-Like-I'm-Fixin'-to-Die Rag" ("Be the first one on your block / To have your boy come home in a box"). Families were splintering under the collective influence of psychedelic drugs, political protests, and the "counterculture," to the consternation of conservatives everywhere; so Provost Leach's lecture, delivered in the heart of the British Establishment, felt to some like a subversive gesture, a call to revolution.

As for me, I wasn't getting on with my father, who had become, among other things, an angry drunk. My sisters and I had been aware of his nocturnal rages, but our mother had done her best to shield us from them. We knew that it was best to avoid him in the evenings. We knew to remain silent at breakfast if his eyes looked red. But we had rarely, if ever, felt the full force of his whiskey wrath. Then, in January 1961, I flew with him to England to begin my boarding-school life, and before the beginning of term we were together in London for several days. We were sharing a hotel room, and I soon learned that Johnnie Walker (Red Label) would be sharing it as well.

Those cold January nights at the Cumberland Hotel were traumatic. I would be shaken awake by my father in the small hours, after he and Johnnie had reached the bottom of a bottle, and he would abuse me in language I'd never heard, words I never suspected that my father would even know, much less use against his eldest child and only son. All I could think about was getting away from him, and I never stopped. When I graduated from Cambridge in 1968, he didn't come to the ceremony, nor did he buy any plane tickets for my mother or my sisters, so I stood alone with my degree on the lawn at King's College among the happy family groups celebrating my fellow graduates.

The source of all our discontents, I thought. Yes, indeed.

I did not return home for long after graduating but chose to make my life in England. For a long time after that, family life—or, rather, finding stability in it—was difficult for me. There were marriages, divorces. My father died, and in the last week of his life there was an important, though all too brief, loving reconciliation. However, this is not the place to intrude too much on such narrow privacies or to spill any tawdry secrets. I'll just say: we would not be who we are today without the calamities of our yesterdays.

By the time I met Eliza, a small, loving family had solidified around me: my two sons, my sister, her two daughters, and a next generation beginning to arrive. This was the heart of my life, all the stronger for the instabilities of earlier years. And all of them loved Eliza immediately. They had not been so enthusiastic about one or two of the women who preceded her. (My son Milan is the kind of young man who says what he really thinks. "Dad," he once asked me, "you have so many amazing women friends, they're all brilliant and warm and impressive and I really like them." Then, after a perfectly timed comic pause: "Why don't you date women like that?")

But when he and all the rest of my family met Eliza, they told me, "Finally." (Eliza then had T-shirts made for me, with FINALLY emblazoned upon them.)

When I met Eliza's family—her father, her three siblings, their partners—it was in the aftermath of their grievous loss, the death of Eliza's mother, Michele. But it was a close, loving family, deeply engaged with one another's lives, and richly talented in many different ways. Eliza is the eldest of four siblings. Her brother Chris became a partner in his law firm before he turned forty and is now the first and only Black man to sit on the bench of the Delaware Supreme Court; her brother Adam is a gifted visual artist and graphic novelist (*Washington White*); her sister, Melissa, has worked successfully in the financial world. Their father, Norman, now retired, was a lawyer too, and a successful local politician in his hometown of Wilmington, Delaware, winning many terms of office.

They all welcomed me into their lives. Norman told Eliza that he had never seen her happier, and if I was the reason, then the relationship was fine by him. Melissa echoed the sentiment. "Take a moment to notice how happy you sound," she told Eliza one day. "You two are doing really well."

Her family liked me! My family liked her! Our happiness was firmly grounded in the good strength that family can give. I left Edmund Leach behind. Family was no longer the source of my discontents.

But.

Was it possible—was it even proper or ethical—to speak of happiness in the middle of a pandemic? We both caught, and luckily recovered from, Covid-19 at the very beginning, in March 2020. It wasn't easy. I got it badly, then Eliza got it too, but in spite of being very ill, she went on caring for me. Afterward she told me, "There were moments when I thought we might not make it, when I thought, maybe this is the end of the story." But we made it. There were people banging pots and pans every evening to celebrate the work of front-line healthcare workers. We joined in to celebrate, also, our own survival.

After that, the exterminating angel was knocking on every door. Nobody then knew how to combat the killer bug. Doctors and nurses were working around the clock, and they were dying too. Hospitals were places where people were going to die. When you were put on a ventilator, there was almost no chance that you would be taken off it and live.

On August 12, 2022, I learned what it was like to be put on a ventilator. It was impossible, then, not to think of the gigantic tragedy of the pandemic, so much greater than my own.

Eliza lost two beloved uncles to the coronavirus. I lost no family members, but one dear friend went early, and many more narrowly survived. My daughter-in-law, Zafar's wife, Natalie, got it badly and was hospitalized, and for a time we feared we might lose her. Her recovery was a huge relief, but it was long and slow. And I couldn't go to London to see my family, nor could they travel to New York to see me, for two years—years that felt like centuries.

Millions died, and here I am chattering about being happy? And beyond the pandemic, a world in crisis. America torn in two by the radical right, the U.K. in dreadful disarray, India sinking fast into authoritarianism, freedom everywhere under attack from the *bien-pensant* left as well as book-banning conservatives, the planet itself in dire straits, refugees, hunger, thirst, and war in Ukraine. To say, at such a historical moment, "I am happy"—wasn't that a luxury? A form of chosen blindness, willful, selfish? Wasn't it exactly what "Henry White," the character in my unfinished story, was guilty of—happiness as a privilege, as unexamined, entitled behavior? Wasn't it a form of turning away from reality into a blinkered cultivating-one's-garden solipsism?

What right did anyone have to claim true happiness in our almost terminally unhappy world?

And yet the heart knew what it knew, and insisted.

———

On Saturday, May 1, 2021, Eliza and I were celebrating our fourth anniversary. The continuing pandemic limited what we could do. We decided on a little staycation at a hotel overlooking the park. They upgraded us to a suite on the twenty-fifth floor, so the view was spectacular. After dinner, she reminded me, hesitantly, that several months earlier I had asked about the size of her ring finger. Was that just for my general information, she wondered, or, after four years, had there been an actual purpose to it?

"Hang on a minute," I said, getting to my feet and heading for the bedroom. "I'll be right back."

My unexplained exit, combined with my expressionless face, worried her. Had she put her foot in it? she wondered. Then I came back and handed her a small purple box and told her that it was the answer to her question. It's one of the very few times that I've taken her completely by surprise.

That's how we got engaged, high in the sky above Central Park, and whatever shape the world might be in, nobody could tell us that we weren't the happiest of people.

"You're my person," she said.

"You're my person," I replied.

———

How to have a private wedding in the age of zero privacy: (1) Don't do it in New York City. (2) Do it in Wilmington, Delaware, where Eliza grew up, and nobody recognizes your name. When we went to get our license, the lady in the office wrote down my name without a flicker of acknowledgment. I had to spell it out letter by letter for her. (3) Invite your friends to a nice lunchtime ceremony and tell them, "No social media."

That's it.

We got married on Friday, September 24, 2021, and all our friends and family knew about it, but it was out of the public eye, and stayed that way for almost a year, and would probably still be private if not for the knife.

It was a beautiful day. The weather, our friends, the ceremony, the joy. We joined our two traditions, garlanding each other (Indian) and jumping over a broomstick (African American). She spoke lyrically to me, poetry being her superpower, and to rise to the occasion I included, in my more prosaic words to her, e. e. cummings's poem "i carry your heart with me(i carry it in":

> i carry your heart with me(i carry it in
> my heart)i am never without it(anywhere
> i go you go,my dear;and whatever is done
> by only me is your doing,my darling)
>   i fear
> no fate(for you are my fate,my sweet)i want
> no world(for beautiful you are my world,my true)
> and it's you are whatever a moon has always meant
> and whatever a sun will always sing is you
>
> here is the deepest secret nobody knows
> (here is the root of the root and the bud of the bud
> and the sky of the sky of a tree called life;which grows
> higher than soul can hope or mind can hide)
> and this is the wonder that's keeping the stars apart
>
> i carry your heart(i carry it in my heart)

My family wasn't at the wedding, because at that time the United States wasn't allowing foreigners into the country on account of the coronavirus. We brought a laptop to the ceremony and set it on a well-placed podium, and they watched it all from London on the new thing called Zoom that had become so essential. Friends and family members spoke, funny and touching. Eliza's poet-sister Aracelis Girmay read a collage text drawn from many poems. After what Hemingway might have called a fine lunch (we ate it gratefully, and it was good), we went to the exquisite Marian Coffin Garden on the grounds of a big house named Gibraltar that now stood empty and run-down—we being Eliza, me, and her family, along with a photographer and a photographer's assistant—and made our wedding-day images. A couple of days later, we went to London and held a small post-wedding celebration for my family and close friends on that side of the water. It felt like the beginning of the rest of my life.

But disaster was waiting for us, less than a year in the future.

———

Milan, Sardinia, Capri, Amalfi, Rome, Umbria. The summer of 2022. After the long pandemic retreat, Italy felt like a miracle, wrapping us in an old friend's warm embrace. Very warm, in fact. There was a heat wave and the rivers ran dry. It was impossible to go outdoors in the midday sun. But Italy renewed us. It took the old used parts of you away, and fresh new parts were born to fill the space. Italy was a smile and a feast. Italy was music. We were there for a month. In Milan we had dinner in an old haunt of mine, the restaurant Rigolo in the Brera neighborhood, and it was nice to be remembered by the owners. In Sardinia, I celebrated my seventy-fifth birthday in the house of dear friends, in a rocky landscape that reminded me of the world of the novel I was just finishing, and our host, Steve Murphy, gave me the birthday gift of singing for me one of my favorite Dylan songs, "Love Minus Zero / No Limit," accompanying himself on his guitar in the star-filled night. In Amalfi and Ravello, there were more old friends, Alba and Francesco Clemente, and the night of the Festival of Sant'Andrea. In 1544, the saint had conjured a storm that destroyed the Saracen fleet that had come to conquer the town, and he was still the patron saint of seagoing folk. First men brought the saint's statue on its palanquin to the water's edge to bless the boats. Then they carried the saint through the streets and finally ran up the steep steps of the cathedral with the saint's palanquin on their shoulders; one false step would have meant disaster, but there was no false step. After the saint there were fireworks, which we watched from the terrace of Alba's house high on the hill above the town square, and it felt like the astonishing explosions were right in front of us. In Rome, it was almost too hot to move, and I bought Eliza a fan (in Milan I had bought her a handbag). In Umbria, we were at a celebrated writers' retreat, Civitella Ranieri, which was housed in a fifteenth-century castle belonging to the Ranieri family. They had another castle, in which they lived, so this was their second-best castle, their spare castle, but that was plenty good enough for us. Good work was done there and many new friends made. During the days we wrote, and in the evening there was good food and wine and conversation deep into the night. I played ping-pong against writers half my age and I did not disgrace myself. One day, we visited Arezzo and looked at the frescoes of Piero della Francesca and paid our respects to the statue of Guido d'Arezzo, who invented the modern system of musical notation, the staves and clefs and the rest of it. I corrected the proofs of *Victory City*, and it felt good.

We came back to America, tore ourselves away from that fine

embrace, because Eliza had created photographic and video im-
agery that formed the visual environment for *Castor and Pa-
tience,* a new opera composed by Gregory Spears with lyrics by
Eliza's friend the poet Tracy K. Smith. The opera was to be pre-
miered in Cincinnati on Thursday, July 21. Cincinnati after an
Italian castle was a fairly radical change of pace, but the pre-
miere went well, and Eliza's work was praised.

After that, our old life had twenty days left to run. I began to
plan a trip to London to see my family. On Thursday, July 28, I
made a few final, last-minute corrections to the proofs of *Victory
City,* and then it was ready for the printers. We saw a few friends.
On Tuesday, August 9, we read that Serena Williams planned to
retire after the U.S. Open. End of an era, we thought, as did
everyone else. That night, I had the dream about being attacked
by a gladiator. On Wednesday, August 10, we went out for a date
night to an Italian restaurant called Al Coro.

The small things of everyday life.

Then, on the morning of Thursday, August 11, I flew alone
from JFK to Buffalo and was driven by a nice lady called Sandra
along the southern shore of Lake Erie to Chautauqua.

———

Our plan had been that Eliza would go to see her family in
Delaware and I would go to London for a week to see mine.
But she had decided to stay in New York and surprise me when
I got home from Chautauqua so that we could have a night
together before separating for family time. Meanwhile, in
London, my sons, Zafar and Milan, my sister Sameen, and my
nieces, Maya and Mishka, were excited about my imminent ar-
rival, and Zafar was telling his not-yet-two-year-old daughter,
Rose, that she would see Grandpa soon and he would come to
her swimming class to watch her splash about. And my publish-

ers at Random House had booked me for a Zoom meeting soon after my return to plan the details of my book launch. Everything felt good.

Then the world exploded.

Eliza's friend Safiya Sinclair called her in the middle of the morning, her voice shaking, to ask if she was all right. That was how Eliza first heard that I had been attacked. Then she was screaming at the television as the crawl line across the bottom of the CNN screen confirmed the news. For what seemed like an eternity, there was very little detailed or reliable information. The phone never stopped ringing. Rumor took the place of Fact and increased her agony. I was dead. I had been punched but not killed. I had gotten to my feet and left the stage and was okay.

In faraway London, which felt suddenly farther away than ever, as if the Atlantic Ocean had grown wider in an instant, my family also scrambled desperately for news, horror on every face. They were calling Eliza and she was calling them and nobody was sure of anything. Zafar's media sources were uncertain at first. I had been stabbed five times, ten times. No, I was all right. No, I had been stabbed fifteen times. It was late afternoon in London, stretching into evening, and as many of my family members gathered at Sameen's house, just to be together, slowly the truth came through.

I had been airlifted to the nearest hospital. There seemed to be very little chance that I would live. The next twenty-four hours would decide it.

In New York City, Eliza was trying to find the fastest way of getting to where I was. Her phone was blowing up. All was pandemonium.

Somebody called her—afterward she couldn't remember who it was—and told her that she had better hurry because I wasn't going to make it. Her world was disintegrating. The loving life we had built over the past five years had come to a violent end. A nightmare had crossed the frontier between dream and reality and come true. Her picture of the world had shattered and lay in pieces on the ground.

In his great book *If This Is a Man*, Primo Levi tells us that "perfect happiness is not attainable," but, he proposes, nor is perfect unhappiness. In that moment, Eliza would have said that he was wrong. Perfect unhappiness was the name of the country in which she now lived.

———

She spoke to our literary agents, Andrew Wylie and Jin Auh. Andrew was crying. We had been friends for thirty-six years, and in the hurricane that hit me after the publication of *The Satanic Verses* and the Khomeini fatwa, he had been my strongest and most loyal ally. We had gone through that war together, and now this? He couldn't bear it. But this was a time for action, not tears. "You have to get up there right now," they told Eliza. By road it would take at least seven hours. She didn't have seven hours. The only solution was a plane.

We are not the kind of people who hire private planes. We don't have that kind of money. But right then money wasn't important. All that mattered was getting there. Use the Amex card and worry about the money later. Andrew and Jin found Eliza a plane. It was waiting at an airfield in White Plains, New York. It would cost over twenty thousand dollars. Never mind.

"Go," they said.

She went, and her sister, Melissa, and Melissa's husband, Eumir Brown, a gentle Brooklyn schoolteacher, went with her.

And all the way she bore the burden of the words she had heard on the phone—*He's not going to make it*—words for which there was no possible consolation.

Meanwhile, in Washington, D.C., her brother Adam and his husband, Jeff Leasure, jumped into their car and began to drive northwest, toward Erie, as fast as they could. And in Wilmington, her brother Chris also jumped into his car and also began to drive as fast as he could.

This was how family behaved. Eliza (who was Rachel to them) was beloved family, of course. But now I was family too, and they would be there for me as well as for her.

———

New York State Police were calling her. Pennsylvania State Police were calling her. The helicopter had taken me across the state line to UPMC Hamot, thirty-five miles from Chautauqua in Erie, Pennsylvania, "the only accredited trauma center in the Erie region," according to its online information, and therefore the place that offered my only chance of survival.

He's not going to make it.

When the plane landed, there were security vehicles everywhere. By now the news was blazing across the world's airwaves. A maximum-security operation had been ordered, at the airport and at the hospital. Eliza, Melissa, and Eumir were put into a police car and driven to Hamot. Nobody said much in the vehicle. *They don't want to tell me he's dead,* Eliza thought. *They are taking me to see my husband's dead body.*

———

I wasn't dead. I was in surgery, with multiple surgeons working on different wounded parts of me simultaneously. My neck, my right eye, my left hand, my liver, my abdomen. The slash wounds on my face—my forehead, cheeks, and mouth—and on my chest. The surgery took something like eight hours.

At the end of it, I was on a ventilator, but I wasn't dead.

I was alive.

One year later, my daughter-in-law, Natalie, sent me some notes she had written, a few weeks after the attack, about the first twenty-four hours. When Zafar heard the news, she said, he looked shattered. "Something had shifted in him." Around midnight in London, Eliza had called them from the hospital. She was with the consultant and put the call on speakerphone. The consultant told them all to prepare for the worst, as there was only a small chance that I would survive. As he described my injuries, Natalie heard Eliza howling with grief. *"No please no."* That night, Zafar and Natalie lay in darkness and "the world felt very heavy, silent and dark." Zafar cried all night. "He sounded like a child wanting to hold his father," Natalie wrote. "He knew that if he went to sleep his father might not be here when he woke up." But the next day Eliza called again. I was awake and alert, although still on the ventilator. She put her phone next to my ear so that Zafar could tell me he loved me. I heard him and wiggled my toes, and when Eliza told him that he cried tears of joy.

Later, we learned that the A. was being held in Chautauqua County Jail, and denied bail. The charges against him were attempted murder and aggravated assault. Later still, Eliza and I met Sherri, an FBI agent who came to visit my hospital room to assure me that the feds were working "around the clock" on the case and aiming to build a terrorism case as well. The feds and the state police came to ask me to give a deposition and professed to be impressed by my memory. They were probably being polite. Later still, we heard that "thirty thousand pieces of evidence" had been found in his New Jersey basement—every item on his laptop, all his texts and emails, we presumed. All that felt very abstract to us—to me. The subject in those first days was simple: survival.

Live. Live.

3

Hamot

When I regained consciousness I was seeing visions. They were architectural. I saw majestic palaces and other grand edifices that were all built out of alphabets. The building blocks of these fantastic structures were letters, as if the world was words, created from the same basic material as language, and poetry. There was no essential difference between things made out of letters and stories, which were made of the same stuff. Their essences were the same. The visions conjured up external walls, great halls, high domes that were both lavish and austere, a Mughal mirror-tiled Sheesh Mahal at one time, and at another a stone-walled place with small barred windows. Something like Hagia Sophia in Istanbul was manifested to me by my unsettled brain, and the Alhambra, and Versailles; like Fatehpur Sikri and the Agra Red Fort and the Lake Palace of Udaipur; but also a darker version of El Escorial in Spain, menacing, puritanical, a nightmare rather than a dream. When I looked closely the alphabets were always present, mirror-glittering alphabets and grim letters of stone, brick alphabets and treasure-letters of diamond and gold. After a while, I understood that my eyes were closed. I was still thinking of my eyes in the plural then.

I opened my eyes—only my left eye, as I half-understood; the right eye was covered by a soft bandage—and the visions didn't disappear but became more ghostly, translucent, and I began to take some notice of my true situation. The first, most pressing, least comfortable discovery was the ventilator. Afterward, when it was removed and I could say things, I said it was like having an armadillo's tail pushed down your throat. And when it was re-moved it was like having an armadillo's tail *pulled out* of your throat. I had survived Covid without needing a ventilator. But here it was. And although my head was very fuzzy I remembered the early days of the pandemic, when very few people came off a ventilator and lived.

I couldn't talk. But there were people sitting in my room. Five, maybe six people. I wasn't good with numbers just then. There were letters floating in the air between me and them. Maybe they, the people, didn't exist. Maybe they were hallucinations too. I was on heavy painkillers. Fentanyl, morphine. They were the probable cause of the alphabet hallucinations. Maybe they were the cause of these phantoms in the room as well.

They weren't phantoms. They were Eliza, Melissa, Eumir, Chris, Adam, and Jeff. By air, by road, they had all arrived in time for me to wake up. I wasn't wearing any eyeglasses—they had been broken during the attack or perhaps during the frenzy that followed it—so the people were out of focus, which was perhaps just as well, because I couldn't see the grim expressions on their faces. They were looking at what I couldn't see: me. My neck and cheek on the right side had been slashed open by the knife and they could see the two sides of the cut being held to-gether by metal staples. There was a long horizontal gash along my neck, under my chin, and that was being held together by staples too. They could see that the whole neck area was grotesquely swollen and darkly bloodied. They could see that the dried blood of the wound in my left hand looked almost like stigmata. Around the wound were bandages, and the hand was held stiffly in a splint. And when the nurse came in to tend to my ruined eye, Eliza and the others saw what looked like a sci-fi movie special effect, the eye hugely distended, bulging out of its socket and hanging down on my face like a large soft-boiled egg. The swelling was so bad that the doctors didn't even know, in those first days, if I still had an eyelid. (I did.) Eliza and the others could see the ventilator pipe in my mouth, and nobody could tell them when, or if, it might be removed. The chest wounds were covered up, but they knew my liver had been damaged and a section of my small intestine had had to be removed. They had been told that my heart had been "bruised." They did not know if I would live, or, if I did, what might be my future state. All that was on their faces, but they were blurry. In my anesthetized half-conscious state, I was just glad they were there.

(For many weeks Eliza refused to let me look into a mirror, so I had no idea how awful I looked. Doctors and nurses would come to inspect me and say, "You're looking much better," and I believed their lies, because I wanted to. Deep into the night in the trauma ward of UPMC Hamot, hearing the night-howls of dying men in other rooms, the biggest question—life or death?—hung in the air, and there was no clear answer.)

Eliza was by my side, refusing to let me see her grief or fear, knowing she had to be loving and strong for me. She said, "Move your foot if you can understand me." When my foot didn't move, she was close to despair. Maybe the knife that went so deep into my eye—as deep as the optic nerve—had damaged my brain as well.

A little later, when I was less woozy and could better understand what was being required of me, I did begin to move my foot, once for yes, twice for no, and even in that groggy condition I could feel the waves of relief washing through the room.

Now that they knew I could understand, they could talk to me. Eumir came and sat near my head and said there was something he wanted to read to me. It was President Biden's statement in response to the attack. Eumir read it slowly and softly into my ear:

Jill and I were shocked and saddened to learn of the vicious attack on Salman Rushdie yesterday in New York. We, together with all Americans and people around the world, are praying for his health and recovery. I am grateful to the first responders and the brave individuals who jumped into action to render aid to Rushdie and subdue the attacker.

Salman Rushdie—with his insight into humanity, with his unmatched sense for story, with his refusal to be intimidated or silenced—stands for essential, universal ideals. Truth. Courage. Resilience. The ability to share ideas without fear. These are the building blocks of any free and open society. And today, we reaffirm our commitment to those deeply American values in solidarity with Rushdie and all those who stand for freedom of expression.

When Death comes very close to you, the rest of the world goes far away and you can feel a great loneliness. At such a time kind words are comforting and strengthening. They make you feel that you're not alone, that maybe you haven't lived and worked in vain. Over the next twenty-four hours I became aware of how much love there was flowing in my direction, a worldwide avalanche of horror, support, and admiration. As well as

President Biden's message, there were strong words from President Macron of France: "For 33 years, Salman Rushdie has embodied freedom and the fight against obscurantism. He has just been the victim of a cowardly attack by the forces of hatred and barbarism. His fight is our fight; it is universal. Now more than ever, we stand by his side." There were similar statements made by other world leaders. Even Boris Johnson, then the British prime minister, who had once written an article saying that I didn't deserve the knighthood I had received in June 2007 "for services to literature" because I wasn't a good enough writer, now found some grudging platitudes. India, the country of my birth and my deepest inspiration, on that day found no words. And, inevitably, there were voices expressing pleasure about what had happened. If you are turned into an object of hate, there will be people who hate you. That had been true for thirty-four years.

Friends were texting me on my phone even though they knew I wouldn't be reading texts. Friends were emailing and leaving voicemail even though they knew it to be futile. They were posting messages to me on Facebook and Instagram. *Please, please, be okay.*

The last thing I'd posted on Instagram was my photograph of the full moon over Lake Chautauqua, taken the night before the attack. "Thinking of you," dozens of people wrote in the comments. "Thinking of you with candles lit in the desert." "You are loved and needed by so many, near and far. We are all rooting for you." "Hoping your strength in adversity once again proves a superpower." "Devastated." "May the stars align to protect you even if the moon didn't." "Get well get well recover come through." "We love you." "We love you." "We love you."

Many people said they were praying for me. Even though they knew I was a godless bastard.

"I thought you were gone," my friend the artist Taryn Simon told me much later. "We all thought you were gone. I thought I'd lost you. It was the heaviest feeling I've ever felt."

And then there were the reactions of ordinary people—readers, nonreaders, people I didn't know, just good people horrified by a bad thing. Sameen read me some of these messages on the phone from London, before she got on a plane to America. I wasn't well enough to take in clearly the scale of what was happening outside my hospital room, but I felt it. I have always believed that love is a force, that in its most potent form it can move mountains. It can change the world.

I understood that the strangenesses of my life had put me at the heart of a battle between what President Macron called "hatred and barbarism" and the healing, uniting, inspiring power of love. The woman I loved and who loved me was by my side. We would win this battle. I would live.

For now this room was the world and the world was a deadly game. To escape the game and return to a wider, more familiar reality, I would have to pass a number of tests, both physical and moral, like the heroes in all the world's mythologies. My health—my life—was the Golden Fleece toward which I was trying to sail. The *Argo*, in this telling, was a bed, and the room was the sea, and the sea was the dangerous world.

At some point in that first twenty-four-hour stretch after the surgery, when my life hung in the balance, I dreamed Ingmar Bergman. To be specific, I saw the famous scene from *The Seventh Seal* in which the Knight, returning home from the Crusades, plays a last game of chess against Death, to stave off for as long as possible the inevitable checkmate. That was me. I was the Knight. And my chess game had deteriorated sharply since my college days.

The trauma center at Hamot was not a quiet place. Because of my presence, the hospital had been placed on full security lockdown, with many guards patrolling. If Eliza wanted to get a sandwich from the canteen, a guard had to accompany her. But up here, in the extreme-trauma zone, things were agonizingly unrestrained. There were loud yells demanding medication from someone in one nearby room, and screams from another room from someone for whom medical attention might have come too late. Sometimes there were sobs. And Eliza, walking the corridors past rooms of dying men, couldn't stop herself from wondering if that would also be my fate. *Are they going to put my husband in a body bag as well?*

It almost happened. Later, when it was clear that I would live, the doctors' relief was palpable too. "When they brought you in from the helicopter," said a member of the surgery team, "we didn't think we could save you."

They did save me, but it was that close.

Another doctor said to me, "You know what you're lucky about? You're lucky that the man who attacked you had no idea how to kill a man with a knife."

A fast-flash memory of his black-clad silhouette, slashing wildly, narrowly failing. But also almost succeeding. My foolish, angry A.

———

In the afternoon of August 13, they decided to remove the ventilator. Out it came, that armadillo's tail, and it was about as comfortable as that sounds. But then, good news. I was able to breathe well by myself. And I opened my mouth and out came words.

"I can talk," I said.

This was the beginning of the fightback. For Eliza, it was the beginning of hope. I was alive, and I could breathe, and the rest of it would come back in time. (We refused to think *maybe*. We refused maybe altogether. There would be no maybe. There was only yes.)

———

Eliza would not leave me alone in my trauma room. The others stayed a few nights in a local hotel before heading back into their interrupted lives. My son Zafar arrived from London, and a couple of days later Sameen arrived as well. They also had rooms in the hotel. But Eliza stayed with me. It wasn't easy. The hospital was in a rough neighborhood, she was told. Not safe for her to walk alone, even a couple of blocks to a Walgreens store to pick up a few supplies.

There was a cushioned ledge that she used for a bed. It must have been very uncomfortable, but it was around now that Eliza went into superhero mode. She showed neither grief nor fear, neither exhaustion nor stress, but only love and strength. In the time of my greatest weakness, she became my—our—unbreakable rock. Everyone who came within range had to answer to her—doctors had to explain their decisions, nurses had to describe how they were about to help me, state police officers from New York and Pennsylvania as well as FBI agents coming to see me had to go through her.

She wanted to check that my hospital expenses would be covered by my NYU health insurance. She got through to an associate dean in the College of Arts and Sciences, a very helpful woman who made sure that the insurance would do what needed to be done. Eliza had already begun to plan for our return to New York. How much would an air ambulance cost? Would that be covered by my insurance? (No. That was too much to ask.) Well, then. Was there a plane we could borrow? As it happened, we did know a few people who owned planes—these people were not

from the literary world—and we also knew one or two people
with access to one or two people who owned planes, and at least
three such people kindly offered their planes to us. But in the
end this option proved too complicated. Where were the planes?
Could they get to us when we needed them? Were they equipped
with medical supplies? Could they accommodate the emergency
medical supplies we would need on the journey, plus a medical
professional who would have to accompany us, plus security per-
sonnel? Also . . . I didn't really want to feel beholden to anyone,
no matter how generous. We decided to do what we could afford.
We would go by road. Eliza found the person in the Hamot system who could help us book an ambulette, and find all the people
we would need to travel in it with us. Eliza started speaking to the
police. Almost immediately the Pennsylvania State Police agreed
to escort us as far as the state line, and New York State Police
agreed to meet us there and accompany us all the way to New
York City. In Manhattan, they would bring me to the rehab place
Eliza was talking to: Rusk Rehabilitation, a part of the NYU Langone hospital system and one of the most highly rated rehab hospitals in the country. She made sure Rusk had room, would make
room, and would have that room ready when we needed it.

"When we needed it" was still more than two weeks away. But
Eliza was on the case.

———

Midnight, August 14 to 15, had always had a special meaning for
me. That was the moment, back in 1947, when India had at-
tained independence from British rule. It was also the moment
at which my fictional character Saleem Sinai, the antihero and
narrator of *Midnight's Children,* had been born. I was in the
habit of calling Indian Independence Day "Saleem's birthday."
But this year Independence Day had a more personal meaning.

Monday, August 15, was Day Three. The day on which it became clear that I would continue to live. Let's say: I would be free to live. Which was the freedom in which, right then, I was most interested.

My brain had begun to work again. I had had two scans and they showed that there was no damage, so my brain had no excuse for not working. This was perhaps the greatest good fortune of all—that the blade that had penetrated so deep failed by perhaps a millimeter to cripple my mental capacities, which meant that, as I recovered, I could go on being me.

I was being weaned off the really powerful painkillers—when you've had your life miraculously saved, you don't want to end up as an opioid addict—and so the visions had stopped, which I regretted. I had become fond of my alphabet palaces and the golden letters floating in the air.

"We need to document this." That was perhaps my first coherent thought. I wasn't sure how Eliza would react to the idea, but she immediately, and emphatically, agreed. "This is bigger than just me," I said. "It's about a larger subject."

What I meant, of course, was freedom, whatever that much-battered word now meant. But I also wanted to think about miracles, and about the irruption of the miraculous into the life of someone who didn't believe that the miraculous existed, but who nevertheless had spent a lifetime creating imaginary worlds in which it did. The miraculous—as well as the A. and his victim—had crossed a state line. It had traveled from Fiction into Fact.

Eliza sent for her camera equipment. It would arrive from New York City two days later, so that by Day Five we could begin to document my physical condition, my recovery, and my thoughts about the attack, my work, my ideas, and the world. Eliza is an accomplished photographer and videographer (as well as a novelist and poet—sometimes I think there may be no limits to her gifts), so we needed no outside help. This would be a thing we would do together. It would be a defiance of death and a celebration of life and love, but also, more prosaically, it would look head-on at the damage.

Even before the cameras were with us, we began to record conversations on her phone.

How are you feeling today, honey. How are you doing, darling. This is Day Four after our lives were changed forever.

You know . . . it's up and down. But I am surrounded by the ones I love. Primarily, you. So I can do it.

We're going to come through this. We have more stories to tell. And what we have is the greatest story, which is love.

That's right.

Today is another good day. Another good day for us, together.

It's thanks to you. You're doing all the work.

You did the biggest thing. You didn't die.

My poor Ralph Lauren suit.

We're going to get you another one. We'll walk right into that Ralph Lauren store and say, Give this man a suit.

I think they just might give me one.

How is your hand, darling.

It's heavy. It feels like I have an extra hand hanging off my arm.

I love you. We're going to come through this.

I love you too.

———

I was in no state to talk about freedom. It was a word that had become a minefield. Ever since conservatives started laying claim to it (Freedom Tower, freedom fries), liberals and progressives had started backing away from it toward new definitions of the social good according to which people would no longer be entitled to dispute the new norms. Protecting the rights and sensibilities of groups perceived as vulnerable would take precedence over freedom of speech, which the Nobel laureate Elias Canetti had called "the tongue set free." This move away from First Amendment principles allowed that venerable piece of the Constitution to be co-opted by the right. The First Amendment was now what allowed conservatives to lie, to abuse, to denigrate. It became a kind of freedom for bigotry. The right had a new social agenda too, one that sounded a lot like an old one: authoritarianism, backed up by unscrupulous media, big money, complicit politicians, and corrupt judges. All of this, the complexities created by new ideas of right and wrong, and my desire to protect the idea of freedom—Thomas Paine's idea, the Enlightenment idea, John Stuart Mill's idea—from these new things, was beyond my power to articulate. My voice was weak and faint. My body was in shock. Talking about miracles was about as much as I could manage.

Eliza told me what many people were saying: "Some greater force protected you."

What was I supposed to do with that information? I had been an atheist all my days, an atheist's son and the father of two more atheists, one who didn't talk much about his atheism (Zafar), the other extremely noisy about it (Milan). Now, suddenly, I was asked to believe that a shielding hand had reached down from the sky and protected an unbeliever's life? What next? If miracles were real, what about the rest of it? Life after death? Heaven and hell? Salvation? Damnation? It was too much.

But for half a century I, who believed in science and reason, who had no time for gods and goddesses, had been writing books in which the laws of science were often subverted and people were telepaths, or turned into murderous beasts at night, or fell thirty thousand feet from an airplane and lived and actually grew horns; books in which a man aged twice as fast as normal, or in which a man began to float just half an inch off the surface of the earth, or in which a woman lived to be two hundred and forty-seven years old.

What had I been up to for fifty years?

I wanted to say: I believe that art is a waking dream. And that imagination can bridge the gulf between dreams and reality and allow us to understand the real in new ways by seeing it through the lens of the unreal. No, I don't believe in miracles, but, yes, my books do, and, to use Whitman's formulation, do I contradict myself? Very well, then, I contradict myself. I don't believe in miracles, but my survival is miraculous. Okay, then. So be it. The reality of my books—oh, call it magic realism if you must—is now the actual reality in which I'm living. Maybe my books had been building that bridge for decades, and now the miraculous could cross it. The magic had become realism. Maybe my books saved my life.

I sounded delirious even to myself. I tried to pull myself together.

"Let's record something," I said.

———

On Day Five, to my surprise, the hapless A. made the mistake of giving an interview from Chautauqua County Jail to Steven Vago and Ben Kesslen of the *New York Post*. He had been charged with attempted murder and aggravated assault and had pleaded not guilty. (Not guilty of a crime witnessed by a large crowd of onlookers? If you say so, I thought. I'm not sure that will fly.) In the newspaper's big-eared, inadequately bearded photograph—actually the booking photo provided to the *Post* by the local sheriff's department—he looked absurdly, almost endearingly young, and in his calm demeanor it was possible to imagine the folly of ignorant youth. I know I did the right thing, his expression tells us, and I don't care who says otherwise.

The article revealed that he had been "inspired" to go to Chautauqua after he saw a tweet "sometime in the winter" announcing my coming participation in the event there. *Thank you,* I thought, *that reveals premeditation.* "When I heard he survived, I was surprised, I guess," he also said. *Thank you again,* I thought; *that reveals intent.* Other than that, there wasn't much of interest in his remarks. He "admired" the Ayatollah Khomeini, and as for his opinion of me, "I don't like the person. I don't think he's a very good person. I don't like him. I don't like him very much." He hadn't read more than "a couple pages" of my work, but he had seen me lecturing on YouTube, and concluded that I was "disingenuous." "I don't like people who are disingenuous like that," he said, somewhat opaquely. Disingenuous like what? He did not elaborate.

"I wanted to murder him because he was disingenuous" would be an unconvincing motive if one were to use it in crime fiction, and my strongest feeling, after reading his remarks, was that his decision to kill me seemed undermotivated. If I were to write a character whose motive for cold-blooded murder—not a *crime passionnel* but something planned and worked out in detail well in advance—was that he had watched a few videos, I suspect my publishers would say that they found the character unconvincing. It may seem bizarre for the almost-murderee to address his almost-murderer reprovingly and say, "You'll have to come up with a better reason than that"—after all, he *had* tried to kill me, so evidently he considered his reasons to be sufficient—but that's what I wanted to do.

I wanted to meet him. I wanted to sit in a room with him and say, "Tell me about it." I wanted him to look me in my (one re-maining) eye and tell me the truth.

Eliza was strongly opposed to this plan. "That's not going to happen," she told me. It wasn't clear that it would be possible anytime soon, anyway, given my state of health; and the A. him-self might refuse. His lawyers would probably advise him against it. At first, however, I was determined to try. But then I thought that the young man's level of intelligence did not appear to be high—"non-rocket-scientific," I may have said to Eliza—or, at least, his powers of self-expression lacked a certain sophistica-tion. It was my unkind guess that this was not somebody who lived an examined life. If I were to mention to him the cele-brated dictum of Socrates, "The unexamined life is not worth living," I doubted that it would elicit an interesting response. I decided that I didn't need to hear his clichés. It would be better for me to make him up.

At that point I had not decided to write this book. We were making our video, audio, and photographic record of what was happening to me—to *us*—but we hadn't even thought whether that should remain private, a sort of diary for ourselves and maybe the family, or whether it could have a more public life. Our decision to make a documentary film, and my decision to write this book as well, happened almost simultaneously, and then I thought: "There are three important characters in this story—Eliza, myself, and *him*." And I decided that imagining him, getting myself inside his head and describing what I found there, would be more interesting to me than confronting him in his black-and-white prison jumpsuit and listening to his ideo-logue's black-and-white ends-and-means garbage. So he will have his chapter. He will get his turn.

I wasn't at all well. I was broken. But I was healing.

The liver is an amazing organ. It regenerates. My liver regenerated and began to work properly. I was able to avoid turning yellow.

My small intestine appeared to be functioning too, so the surgeons had done well. What makes hospitals happiest is when the patient says he is having bowel movements. Hospitals really don't like it when your bowels are not moving and they give you medication that causes diarrhea and you ask them to please stop and you promise in pleading tones that your bowels will move soon, they really will, and then, finally, they do move, and everyone cheers up.

Fluid was inexplicably gathering under my right lung. It needed to be drained. I was taken out of my room to an operating theater on a lower floor. I had to lie on my side, a local anesthetic was applied, and then there was a needle, and the draining began.

"Don't worry. I'm the champion at draining fluids," the doctor told me. Oh, I thought (but did not say), I didn't know there was a championship? A World Series of fluid draining? A Super Bowl of fluid draining? Who would perform the halftime show? Muddy Waters? Aqua? Shut up, Salman. It will be over soon. It took longer than I'd thought it would and there was a lot of fluid. Over nine hundred cc's! The champion held up his trophy, a plastic bag full of a bright pinkish-reddish substance. "I hadn't realized it would be so colorful," I said. That's because I hadn't thought that there would be blood mixed up with whatever that fluid was. But of course there was blood.

———

While I was out of the room, Eliza turned the camera on herself and let her feelings out, the ones she refused to let me see, the grief, the fear, the bewilderment, the sense of having come loose from what she had thought to be her life, and, and above all, her fury at the man "who came to Chautauqua and chose violence. He chose violence." But, she said, "I'm okay, I'll be okay, because he didn't die. My husband lived."

It was a long time before she allowed me to watch the recording of her soliloquy, her rant. When I did see it, I was overwhelmed by the evidence of her suffering and understood even more deeply the immense effort she had made to hide it, and smile, and care for me with love. She had to recover from that. She had been wounded almost as badly as I had.

My tongue had a deep cut in it, on the left side. When I fell at the amphitheater I must have accidentally bitten it. Stitches were required. Eliza said that watching me holding my mouth open while a doctor took a threaded needle and sewed up my tongue was the second-worst thing she had to watch. The stitches were self-dissolving and would be gone in less than two weeks, I was told. Until then I would be on a soft diet—soup, puréed potatoes, not much else. I consoled myself with the thought that at least my teeth seemed fine; they hadn't fallen out, as I had been sure they would after the first blow.

Gradually, on the predicted schedule, my tongue healed, and the stitches fell away.

The worst thing Eliza had to watch was my eye. A nurse had to come in every hour to moisten it with saline solution, because it was so distended, bulging out so far, that it was impossible for the eyelid to close, so the eye couldn't moisturize itself. There was plenty to cry about, but there were no tears.

When the bandages were removed, the eye was a monstrosity. Doctors came to test it to see if there was any vision left at all. I was told to put my uninjured right hand over my left eye, and then they shone a light into the right eye. There was one time when, with great excitement, I said I could see the light at the edge of my right eye's field of vision. The doctors got excited too, but it was a false hope. I just hadn't covered up my left eye well enough, and that was the eye that could see the light, around the edge of my hand.

The eye was lost. I was trying to come to terms with that. The optic nerve had been damaged, and that was that. He didn't get me, the A., but he got my eye. Even now, writing this, I still haven't come to terms with the loss. It's difficult physically—to be unable to see a whole quadrant of one's normal field of vision is hard to handle, also to lose two-eyed perspective, so that when I try to pour water into a glass it's easy to miss the glass—but it's even more difficult emotionally. To accept that this is how it's going to be for the rest of my life . . . it's depressing. But, as Saleem Sinai's parents repeatedly told him during his childhood in *Midnight's Children* (and as mine told me), "What can't be cured must be endured."

The day came when the doctors told me their short-term plan for the eye. No final decision could be made about its long-term future until the swelling had gone down, they said. The swelling was going down, but there was a long way to go. However, in a few days it might be possible to pull the eyelid down over the eye, and once that was possible, there was a way of easing its difficulties and protecting it better. They proposed to lower the eyelid and then stitch it shut. After that the tear ducts would start working again and the eye wouldn't need the hourly saline moisturization. And the eye would be safe from further harm. (What further harm could there be, I wondered, but, once again, forbore to ask.)

"That sounds really painful," I said.

"We'll use a strong local anesthetic," I was assured.

"Okay," I said. "Because I'm really not very good about pain."

The procedure followed a couple of days later. I saw the approach of the needle and said, fearfully, "What about the anesthetic?" I was told it was in the needle. All I can say about what followed is that, if that was true, I can't begin to imagine how painful the procedure would have been if it wasn't. Eliza was in the room, so she heard my loud noises of anguish, and saw my body stiffen. Let me offer this piece of advice to you, gentle reader: if you can avoid having your eyelid sewn shut . . . avoid it. It really, really hurts.

It was "successful," as medical folks say. It's not the word I would have chosen myself. It was the closest thing to unbearable pain I had ever experienced—yes, including the knife blows; I was in so much shock during the attack that I didn't experience that pain as pain, even though those witnesses I mentioned reported that I had been "wailing." After this "successful" procedure I thought of lines from Bob Dylan's "Love Minus Zero / No Limit," which my friend Steve sang to me on the night of my birthday in Sardinia in June: ". . . *there's no success like failure / and that failure's no success at all.*"

It would be seven weeks before the stitches could be cut away.

———

On Day Seven at 11 A.M., Eliza's laptop was set in front of me so that I could watch friends and allies gathering on the steps of the New York Public Library to declare their solidarity. Exactly one week earlier, I had been lying on the floor at the Chautauqua amphitheater, thinking about dying, trying not to die. Now here were hundreds of people gathered on Fifth Avenue "standing with Salman." Here was my friend the wonderful novelist Colum

McCann saying of me, *"Je suis Salman,"* just as I and many others had said, after the murders of the *Charlie Hebdo* cartoonists on January 7, 2015, *"Je suis Charlie."* How moving it felt, but also strange, to become the slogan.

Suzanne Nossel, CEO of PEN America, the writers' organization of which I was an ex-president, made passionate opening remarks. "When a would-be murderer plunged a knife into Salman Rushdie's neck, he pierced more than just the flesh of a renowned writer. He sliced through time, jolting all of us to recognize that horrors of the past were hauntingly present. He infiltrated across borders, enabling the long arm of a vengeful government to reach into a peaceful haven. He punctured our calm, leaving us lying awake at night contemplating the sheer terror of those moments on stage at Chautauqua. And he shattered our comfort, forcing us to contemplate the frailty of our own freedom." This speech, and all that followed, brought me close to tears, but I also thought, *Don't give him so much power, Suzanne. We aren't so easily shattered. Don't make him sound like an angel of doom. He's just a dumb clown who got lucky.*

Over a dozen speakers, including dear friends—Kiran Desai, Paul Auster, A. M. Homes, Francesco Clemente. Emotion overwhelmed me. It was hard to speak. But afterward Eliza turned on her camera and asked me about it.

How did you feel, darling, seeing everyone gathered there for you on a beautiful sunny day in New York.

My voice was frail and my breath uneven. I spoke in broken phrases.

I felt . . . grateful . . . I was moved . . . to know . . . that my life . . . meant . . . meant so much . . . to people. And I was . . . happy . . . to hear my work . . . read out.

After the event at the library there were meetings in my support everywhere, or so it seemed—in England, Canada, and all over Europe. I thought again that love was a real force, a healing force. I have no doubt at all that the love coming toward me— the love of strangers as well as family and friends—did a great deal to help me come through.

In the beginning . . . back then . . . after the fatwa . . . there was quite a lot of hostility, even from the literary world . . . I have the feeling . . . that maybe now . . . people like me . . . a little bit.

All I've ever tried to do . . . is good work . . . and the right thing. That's all I've ever . . .

Later that day, I needed to tell Eliza how grateful I was to her, too. "You're really going the extra fucking mile."

She told me I didn't need to thank her.

"But I feel deep gratitude . . . I want you to know . . . that I feel it."

She changed the subject, and asked about a Belafonte calypso she had heard me humming.

"Jackass Song," I said. " 'Now I tell you in a positive way / Don't tie me donkey down there.' "

She asked me to sing it. I can't sing at the best of times, but I sang for her in my faint, broken voice. "*Now me donkey gone mad they say / Don't tie me donkey down there / 'Cause he high on a bale of hay / Don't tie me donkey down there!*"

Makes me happy, I told her, talking to you about silly things.

———

The event on the library steps gave me a big energy boost, better than any medicine. I talked to Eliza about how we had to get our life back.

One has to find life, I said. *One can't just sit about recovering from near death. One has to find life.*

—————

I am trying to remember if I ever felt angry in those days. I was in the extreme-trauma ward at Hamot for eighteen days—eighteen of the longest days of my life—and as I try to put myself back in that room I can recall feeling weak, determined, exhausted, depressed, stunned, sick, groggy, and, in the company of Eliza, Zafar, and Sameen, also loving and loved. I don't remember anger. I think that anger felt like a wasteful luxury to me. It wasn't useful, and I had more important matters to attend to. I didn't think very much about the man whose actions had put me in this place, or about the men whose murderous ideology inspired him to act as he did. I thought only about survival, by which I meant not only staying alive, but getting my life back, the free life I had so carefully built over the last twenty years.

My battered body was doing quite well, all things considered. I learned a lot in those days about the astonishing ability of the human body to repair itself. The human animal is capable of many damaging (and a few noble) actions, but when its existence is threatened a powerful instinct kicks in and takes charge. It was that survival instinct that had whispered in my ear as I lay bleeding in Chautauqua. *Live. Live.* It was still whispering to me in my hospital bed.

As for the rest of it—getting my old life back—I knew that would have to wait. This would be a long journey, and before I could go down that road I had to learn to walk.

There was an armchair next to the bed. The first step was to feel able to sit in that chair. I found that at first I needed help moving my legs around, help sitting up, help sitting down. But it was good to be more upright, and every day it became just a little easier to move myself toward the chair. Every day I was a little more able to do things for myself. The day I was able to make it to the toilet, do my good-patient business of emptying my bowels, and then clean myself without a nurse's help—well, that felt like a liberation. I had been terrified that I would be the kind of invalid who needs someone to wipe him, to wash him, to treat him like a baby. I began, just a little, to think I might soon be a grown-up once again.

There was no mirror in the bathroom. I still hadn't seen my face.

After about ten days, I walked out of the room! There was a nurse by my side and I had, that first time, a walking frame—what the British call a Zimmer frame—but I managed to make it halfway down the hotel corridor and back again. Security guards and hospital staff gave me encouraging thumbs-up signs. And after that, every day I walked a little better.

Being able to do a few simple everyday things for myself lifted my spirits greatly. I had to learn how to hold a toothbrush and squeeze toothpaste onto it, using only one hand. But worrying medical issues remained. There were small bags attached to various parts of my body to catch fluids that were leaking out of me. And one of the knife wounds in my face had damaged the channel by which saliva reached my mouth, and the saliva was oozing out of my cheek. A young doctor came to attend to this. He pushed a strip of absorbent fabric into my face and would visit twice a day to press hard on the wound to pull some of the strip out, soaked in saliva. Slowly the leak dried up. The procedure was extremely uncomfortable, and I began to call him Dr. Pain. But it worked, and by the time I left Hamot the saliva wasn't dripping out of my face anymore.

My left hand was being held immobile in its splint. It was too early to begin any physical therapy; the tendons needed to repair themselves first. Along with my blinded right eye, this crippled hand was the most unavoidable evidence of my new reality. More than one person tried to reassure me by saying, "At least you're right-handed," but that well-meaning thought didn't really comfort me. My main source of comfort was the presence by my side of Eliza, Zafar, and Sameen.

Zafar had been nine years old at the time of the fatwa and had had to grow up with that menace hovering over his father's head. Then, just as things seemed to be improving, his beloved mother, Clarissa, died of a savagely aggressive recurrence of breast cancer after over five years' remission. He was nineteen. He had come through the ordeal of such a childhood with grace and poise, and it was just too bad, I thought, that after more than twenty years the past should come back to haunt him and bring him from London to this faraway place where his father lay fighting for his life. I was by no means the only person whose days had been deformed by the terrorist threat. He was a victim too.

———

Sameen and I had been the closest of allies ever since the day she first showed up in Bombay, one year and two weeks after I did. Nobody had been closer to me during childhood. She fought with people for me if she thought they were being mean, and I got her out of trouble with our parents. One day when we were perhaps eight and nine years old the doorbell rang. An irate parent stood there and raised his voice at my father. "Your daughter just beat up my son!" My father started laughing. "Shh," he replied. "Don't say that so loud."

We had remained close all our lives. And now this. I told her over and over how much I loved her and how much it meant to me—how much it was helping me—that she had come. After a few days she said, "This is confusing. You've never been so nice to me." This was our way—teasing, joking, sending each other up, knowing that our love didn't need to be stated sentimentally in order to exist. And here I was being tearfully sentimental. She was right to be confused: it was totally out of character.

"I'm always nice to you," I protested.

"No, you're not," she said, happily. "Not like this."

Before Sameen arrived at Hamot, Eliza had shown her my wiggling toes on her iPhone, to reassure her that my brain was functioning. When she arrived, she began doing for me what we had both done for our mother when we were young and she lay tired in bed in the afternoon: she kneaded my feet (and massaged those talkative toes) to soothe me. *Dabao,* I said to her in Urdu, echoing our mother's old command. "Press." For a week our lifelong intimacy brought me, if not joy, then at least the memory of joy. Then, on Day Eight, she went back to London, finding it hard to leave, angry at herself for not having booked a more distant departure date. On Day Nine, Zafar went home too. After that it was just Eliza and me, and there were nine more days to go.

———

When he heard the news about me, Milan's only thought was to get to my bedside as fast as he could. However, the Atlantic Ocean stood in his way, and at twenty-five he was in the grip of an acute fear of flying. He hadn't been able to get on a plane for almost six years. All that day, August 12, he was stuck, painfully, on the horns of this dilemma. I confess that I didn't entirely understand the source of his fear, because for much of his young life he'd flown everywhere, both to me in New York and with me to, for instance, India, Cyprus, and Rome. Spending time with him had always been one of my highest priorities, and until the fear arrived we had alternated between my visits to London and his trips to America. But then the fear arrived as if from nowhere, and after that, for a long time, I was the one who had done all the traveling. And now the attack was asking him a question he didn't know how to answer. Yes, he would fly immediately!—No, he couldn't do it.—Yes, he would make himself do it.—No, he would get to the airport but he wouldn't be able to board the plane.

His mother, Elizabeth—Elizabeth West, Lady Berkeley, now happily married to the composer Michael Berkeley, and still a good friend—came to the rescue. She bought him a transatlantic passage on the *Queen Mary* 2, the one remaining passenger liner crisscrossing the ocean. It would sail from Southampton on a seven-day journey to New York and would arrive at the end of August. It was lucky she moved so swiftly and so generously, understanding (as Eliza had understood when she paid for the private flight to Erie) that there are moments in life when you don't calculate, you just do it. Twenty-four hours after she got Milan his berth, the voyage had sold out.

In my hospital bed, hardly able to move, I heard about Milan's boat ride, and my first reaction was envy. Long before the attack I had watched a Meryl Streep movie, *Let Them All Talk,* most of which happened aboard that very ship. I remembered thinking that the movie wasn't much, but the boat looked amazing.

I spoke to Milan before he sailed. "I want to go on that boat too," I said. "Maybe when I'm better we can do it together."

"Yes, Dad," he said. "You'll get better and we'll go."

It felt good to dream about a happier future.

———

At the Day Fifteen mark, I was walking up and down the hospital corridors without assistance. I was much less frail in voice and body. The army of doctors that inspected various parts of me during the course of each day expressed satisfaction, even surprise. The top man, a surgeon with the improbably gastronomic name of James Beard, said it might soon be time to send me off to rehab. The good people at Rusk in Manhattan said they were ready for me. The ambulette was ready. "Just a couple more days," I was told.

My stitched-up eye was doing okay. My left hand was still immobile in its splint, but I was told they would remove that at Rusk and begin physical therapy. The little bags attached to my body were taken away, because nothing was leaking into them anymore. Hopefully, no more liquid would collect beneath my lung. All the stab wounds and gashes seemed to be closed. Even Dr. Pain didn't need to squeeze any more saliva out of my face. Dr. Eye, Dr. Hand, Dr. Stabbings, Dr. Slash, Dr. Liver, Dr. Tongue—all began to sign off.

"I think we can take the staples out," I was told by Dr. Staples on Day Seventeen. "Everything seems to have healed pretty well."

"When they are out," I asked, "can I shave?" I had seventeen days' growth of beard hair around the wounds in my neck and face. It felt itchy and uncomfortable.

"Not for a while," said Dr. Staples. "Give it a couple of weeks."

Snip-snip went the cutters, and the metal staples fell out. Some snips were painless, others stung, but all of them felt good. At least I wasn't being artificially held together anymore.

One of the doctors brought me a gift of chocolates from the "best artisan chocolatier in Erie." Another brought Eliza and me hot dogs, also the best in town. Nurses rustled up eyepatches for me to try on. They weren't comfortable, but the thought was kind. Everyone was happy. One of the nurses told Eliza, "Very few people walk out of here." Meaning, most leave in body bags.

Day Eighteen. I was wearing clothes, rather than a hospital smock, for the first time since I arrived . . . a T-shirt, tracksuit pants, sneakers. I was to be taken in a wheelchair through the hospital to a discreet loading bay where, we hoped, there would be no media attention. We didn't want it to be known that I was being moved to New York City. We wanted a media blackout, to let me recover quietly, without prying eyes or ears.

Time to go.

4

Rehab

New York City in the late afternoon, shining in the sunlight. It did my heart good to see it again, its *jolies-laides* streets both generous and mean, so much talent in the air, so many rats underfoot, its people striding forth in summer shorts, its parks brightened by young girls in flower, its rusting metal bridges, its pinnacles, its terrible road surfaces, its everything-at-once-ness, its inexhaustible abundance, its crowded excess, and construction sites and music everywhere. Home. As the ambulette moved through Manhattan I had the feeling of being back in my right place. I had left this busy sanctuary nineteen days ago and been trapped in a paradox: almost killed in the misleadingly peaceful gentleness of one distant place, and then saved in another far-away neighborhood of unsafe streets. Every minute of my time at Hamot I had felt like a fish out of water, in spite of the skill of surgeons and the kindnesses of nurses. I have always been a big-city boy—Bombay, London, New York. Cities' stories were my story too, and here again was my preferred ocean, this story-sea of concrete and steel in which I had always preferred to swim.

Arriving at Rusk was somewhat macabre, because everyone was anxious that I not be seen, preferring an anonymous arrival that didn't alert the news media to my presence in the city, for security reasons. So Eliza put a scarf over my face, and my stretcher was brought out of the ambulette and placed on a gurney, and I was wheeled anonymously through unknown space. It felt a little too much like being dead. I tried to brush that thought aside as I was brought scarf-faced into an elevator and up to a room and then the scarf was removed. This first room had nowhere for Eliza to sleep, even though she had arranged with Rusk that that would be possible; we had to wait and then move to a second room.

I was back in the city, on Seventeenth Street and Second Avenue, and yet I wasn't really back, because I couldn't tell anyone I was there. My feelings of elation evaporated. Once again I felt dragged back into the ugly past, the days of being "in hiding" in Britain, living at "undisclosed locations" with armed police officers, far from everyone I loved. There were armed police officers outside this room as well. But at least Eliza was inside it, and Milan was on his way. The *Queen Mary 2* had arrived in New York the day before. Eliza's sister, Melissa, had met Milan off the boat. We had rented an Airbnb place for him on the Upper East Side. Our home was a question mark. Eliza had arranged for ADT security services to come and give the place a serious security upgrade—cameras, panic buttons, all of that. I thought it was better that Milan not stay there. For one thing, the block was newly infested by paparazzi. Melissa drove him to his rented apartment and he settled in, and then, the next day, I arrived and he came to see me. Before he entered my room, Eliza sat with him in a small visitors' room and told him what to expect—my injuries, my fatigue, and the rest.

It was an emotional reunion. My energy level was low, but I

was overjoyed to see him. He told me later that he had dealt with most of his grief and fear about what happened to me during his long solitary passage across the ocean, so that by the time he arrived in my room at Rusk he could just be happy to see me, and to see that I was chatty, telling jokes, "still being Dad." I'm glad he never saw the worst of it, although he was distressed by the bandaged eye, the hand in its splint, the scarred chest, which he wanted to see even though (or because) I told him that the scars made my torso look like a subway map. It was enormously uplifting for me to have him there, and for him to see, as he told me, that I could get up and walk.

Optimism flooded through me—optimism, my great weakness or my great strength (depending on whom you asked and on my own mood as well). In Voltaire's *Candide* (whose full title is *Candide, ou l'Optimisme*), the hero's positivity in the face of the world's horrors is close to idiotic. (If this is the best of all possible worlds, then those parallel universes must be hellish indeed.) When I wrote my novel *Quichotte* I lampooned my own nature by making my title character an optimist of the Candidean kind. And now, bedridden and gravely injured as I was, I began to believe that the worst was past, that Milan's arrival was a sign that a corner had been turned, and happy days would soon be here again.

A bell rang to signal the end of visiting hours, and Milan left for the night. Soon afterward my bladder informed me that my optimism was premature.

There's no elegant way to put this. I had been having trouble urinating. I would feel the urge and reach for the bedside urinal, but then there was a blockage. There would be considerable discomfort, but not much else. They brought in a machine that could find out how full the bladder was. It was dangerously full, they said. What followed is almost too awful to describe.

My first catheter.

Dear reader, if you have never had a catheter inserted into your genital organ, do your very best to keep that record intact. I had passed my seventy-fifth birthday without having this vile ignominy inflicted on me, but here it was. Let me just say that the noises coming out of my mouth during the procedure were sounds I had never heard before. It was my penis begging for mercy.

Not to linger too long upon this issue: The urination problems continued. The urge to urinate, the near impossibility of doing so, the discomfort of trying and failing, the bladder filling up. I began to dread the periodic visits of Nurse Bladder with her Bladderometer. And I had good reason to dread them.

There was a second catheter experience during my time at Rusk.

And a third.

Only then did one of the doctors, Dr. Genius, begin to wonder if something in the cocktail of pills and injections I was being given at regular intervals might be causing the problem. He even identified the medication—I thought of it as Evilomycin—that was the probable culprit. They stopped giving it to me, and within hours there was a transformation. It felt as if a dam inside me had opened its sluice gates. And what had felt nearly impossible suddenly became easy again.

When a patient discovers that it's the medicine that's making him sick, frustration can boil over. I tried to keep my feelings under control, but I may have partially failed to do so. The nurses were understanding. Nurse Bladder kept checking up on me, but now the news from the Bladderometer was good. Everyone was relieved. And nobody apologized for prescribing the Evilomycin.

(A medical condition caused by medication is an *iatrogenic*

KNIFE   83

disorder. Excellent term for a not-excellent thing. I learned it from Martin Amis's wife, Isabel Fonseca. Martin had found it, of course.)

I wasn't completely in the clear, however. The medicine-induced problem had created a secondary problem: a severe urinary-tract infection. At least two weeks on antibiotics would be necessary to get rid of that.

———

Milan had been researching knife attacks. "Dad," he said, sitting by my bed, "there are so many cases where somebody gets stabbed just once and dies. And you got stabbed like fifteen times and you're still alive."

I nodded. "You know," I told him, "the fictional character with whom I now most strongly identify is Wolverine." The X-Man with the superheroic "healing factor."

That got a laugh. "Yeah, but without the claws, Dad."

Now that Milan was with us, Eliza could take some time off. She had barely left my side since her arrival in Erie, but now she could have a bit of a break—she and Milan could take turns at my bedside. The day at Rusk had a full timetable, physical therapy alternating with occupational therapy, with inspections by doctors and nurses in between. It was around four o'clock in the afternoon when the day's work was finally done. Milan came to see me for the afternoon shift, and Eliza arrived later.

We had also decided that the "bed" provided for Eliza was too small, too rudimentary, too uncomfortable for her to use. "It's crazy for you to have to try and sleep there," I said, "when your own bed at home is just a taxi ride away."

She was worried about going home. "What about the paparazzi?" she said.

"Fuck the paparazzi," I said. "Get a good night's sleep."

After that I was alone at night. I was trapped in a bed that had an alarm switched on so it would scream if I tried to get out of it unaided. This did not feel like freedom. My whole world had shrunk down to the size of this screaming bed, and hospital beds were not really for sleeping in. They were for keeping you in your place while people came in and out at all hours to check your vital signs, draw blood, feed you medication, and ask you how you were feeling. Why the police officers sitting outside your room felt that 3 A.M. was the best time to tell one another risqué jokes, and then laugh raucously, was unclear. Why the best time to draw blood was 4 A.M. was not explained to me. Why Nurse Eye needed to come in and turn on bright overhead lights to change my bandage at 5 A.M. was likewise unexplained. By 5:30, the hospital was fully awake, its day had begun, and I could forget about sleep.

As can readily be gleaned from the above paragraph, I was beginning to go a little stir-crazy. Outside my window, seven floors below me, I could hear the music of the city: the ambulances, the fire trucks, the police sirens, the SUVs with their windows rolled down blaring hip-hop to the heavens, drunken revelers laughing and weaving their way home. These familiar sounds pleased me, but also underlined a melancholy fact: I was in my city but not, as yet, fully a part of it. The knife had severed me from my world, cut me brutally away, and placed me in this screaming bed.

During those empty sleepless nights, I thought a lot about The Knife as an idea. When a knife makes the first cut in a wedding cake, it is a part of the ritual by which two people are joined together. A kitchen knife is an essential part of the creative act of cooking. A Swiss Army knife is a helper, able to perform many small but necessary tasks, such as opening a bottle of beer. Occam's razor is a conceptual knife, a knife of theory, that cuts through a lot of bullshit by reminding us to prefer the simplest available explanations of things to more complex ones. In other words, a knife is a tool, and acquires meaning from the use we make of it. It is morally neutral. It is the misuse of knives that is immoral.

Whoa, I told myself. A hard pause. Wasn't that the same thing as saying "Guns don't kill people, people kill people"? Was I falling into a familiar trap?

No. Because a gun had only one use, one purpose. You couldn't cut a cake with a Glock, or cook with an AR-15, or open a bottle of beer with James Bond's favorite Walther PPK. A gun's only way of being in the world was violence; its sole purpose was to cause damage, even to take lives, animal or human. A knife was not like a gun.

Language, too, was a knife. It could cut open the world and reveal its meaning, its inner workings, its secrets, its truths. It could cut through from one reality to another. It could call bullshit, open people's eyes, create beauty. Language was my knife. If I had unexpectedly been caught in an unwanted knife fight, maybe this was the knife I could use to fight back. It could be the tool I would use to remake and reclaim my world, to rebuild the frame in which my picture of the world could once more hang on my wall, to take charge of what had happened to me, to own it, make it mine.

But was that just a consoling lie I was telling myself? Just meaningless bombast? Did I even want to fight back? There were moments—frequent moments in that oppressive bed— when I felt I'd been fighting for most of my life and maybe the universe was telling me I didn't have to do it anymore, I could just stop. I could cry uncle and admit defeat. Maybe that was the message of the knife. *Victory City* would be out in February. My twenty-first book: I was proud of it. I hoped it might be well received. Perhaps that would be as good a time as any to stop, the best exit line I would ever have. Maybe it was time to take the Philip Roth road out of literature and stick a Post-it note on my computer that read "The struggle is over." In this best of all possible worlds, *il faut cultiver notre jardin.* Not that I knew anything about gardening, or wanted to learn.

My first visitor, other than family, was my agent and friend Andrew Wylie. Andrew looks stern but he is an emotional man, and he was close to tears as we embraced. Andrew is a loyal, warmhearted, very intelligent, and very funny man, very different from "the Jackal," the nickname the book trade has given him. (I think he likes it. It makes him sound dangerous.) He was clear about the best way forward.

"I don't know if I can write again," I told him.

"You shouldn't think about doing anything for a year," he said, "except getting better."

"That's good advice," I said.

"But eventually you'll write about this, of course."

"I don't know," I replied. "I'm not sure that I want to."

"You'll write about it," he said.

———

The bathroom attached to my room at Rusk had a mirror. For the first time in several weeks, I could take a look at my face. I told the nurse who had guided me into the toilet that I was fine being by myself, shut the door, and faced the looking-glass. Earlier that morning, a second Dr. Staples, a New York Staples, M.D., taking over from the Erie version, told me there were still a few staples left in my neck, hidden by the growth of beard there, and he took them out. So the face I saw in the mirror was at least free of bits of metal holding it together. The wounds had all closed.

A man sees his reflection and isn't sure he recognizes himself. Who are you, he asks the figure in the mirror. Do I even know you? Will you at some point turn back into me or is this what I'm stuck with now, this wild-haired one-eyed demi-stranger? *"I'm looking through you,"* the Beatles sang. *"Where did you go?"* The man in the toilet talks to the man in the mirror. Are you the ghost of my future? The lips of his reflection do not move. Are you somebody they have brought in to be my replacement? the toilet man asks the mirror man. They think I've been miscast in this role, don't they? They found somebody else, right. They have brought a dead man back to life and given him my scenes. I will be discarded and it will be you instead, and then what happens to me? Where do I go? What about my story arc? How is that resolved?

The lips of the man in the mirror do not move. There is a slash across the top of his forehead. There is a cut in the left-hand corner of his mouth. He is heavily, messily unshaven. His right eyelid is stitched shut. He is successful in moving his bowels. He is successful at cleaning and wiping himself. His one eye looks sad. His face looks shocked. He is playing his part well.

The man in the toilet reaches his hand out toward the surface of the mirror, his undamaged right hand. The surface feels soft, like a thick liquid. His hand passes through it, and then the rest of his body is drawn through as well. Now he is the man beyond the mirror and the mirror is behind him and dark. He is the stranger who has to play his part.

In the looking-glass world, the other, toilet-world can't be seen. The rectangle of the mirror is dark, like a movie screen before the movie begins. Then the movie begins. He is in the children's room of his family home in Bombay, aged seven or so, lying on a bed reading aloud from a book. His sisters pay rapt attention. The book is *Peter Pan*. He knows this scene. It's a photograph taken by his father with a Rolleiflex camera. Sameen and he both have blowups of the picture on the wall at home. It's a childhood idyll that masks the truth.

The image changes. The book is closed and it's later at night. They are listening to their parents' night noises, muffled by closed doors. His father shouting. His mother's tears.

The image changes again. He's not a child anymore. He's a teenager. It's daytime and his father is abusing his mother and he does something he never knew he could do. He goes up to his father and slaps him hard across the face. Then, immediately, he thinks, *Oh God, now he'll hit me back*. His father was not a tall man but he was very strong. *Oh God, he'll break my jaw*. But his father walked away and left him unhurt. Could it be that he felt ashamed?

Now he is thirty-four years old and the author of a successful book, and his father is threatening to divorce his mother because of this book. The portrait of the father in the book has offended his father, because the book-father has a drinking problem. *You put him up to it*, his father accuses his mother. *How would he have dared otherwise? How would he have known all this?* He wants to tell his father, *Children can hear through closed doors*. He wants to tell his father, *If I had really wanted to get you, I would have put in all the stuff I left out*.

He leaves his family home and never returns to it until the week of his father's death. The mirror is dark again.

———

There is the rehab of the body, but there is also the rehab of the mind and spirit. When I left my family home for London, it was the first time I passed through the looking-glass and had to rediscover and remake—rehabilitate—myself in another reality, and play a new role in the world. After the Khomeini fatwa, I had to do it again. When I left London for New York, it was the third time. And this, now, here at Rusk, was the fourth.

"Are you okay in there?" the nurse wants to know.

"Yes. I just need some time."

"No rush. Pull the cord when you're done."

———

That first rehab.

Gumption, Pirsig tells us in *Zen and the Art of Motorcycle Maintenance,* is what the spirit needs to get itself into a good place, and the spirit acquires gumption by being in contact with Quality:

> I like the word "gumption" because . . . it describes exactly what happens to someone who connects with Quality. He gets filled with gumption . . .
>
> A person filled with gumption doesn't sit around dissipating and stewing about things. He's at the front of the train of his own awareness, watching to see what's up the track and meeting it when it comes.

For a long time after I left my parents' home to make a life in London I wasn't at the front of the train of my own awareness. I had a job, but it wasn't a job I wanted. I tried to write, but wrote nothing worth reading. Even when I published a novel, a lot of it soon felt wrong to me. I didn't hear myself in most of its sentences, and I wasn't sure what or who the self I was trying to hear might actually be. In those days I often asked my bathroom mirror who I was, and the mirror didn't have an answer. Only after I found my way into the book that became *Midnight's*

Children—a book in which I tried to reclaim not only India but myself, set in a city, Bombay, much of which was built on land reclaimed from the sea—did I "connect with Quality," and after that, self-knowledge arrived, and the gumption tank filled up. I didn't want to repair any motorcycles, but I learned that, through literature, I could repair myself.

———

The second rehab.

After the fatwa, and the subsequent decade of semi-underground life under police protection, I came close to losing myself again, and, for a while, I floundered. The danger was real; the widespread hostility was almost worse than that. The reason I was not only consoled by the flood of good feeling that came my way after the knife attack, but also surprised by it, was that after the fatwa there was some similar support, but also a hurtful quantity of sharp criticism. In the West there were many voices—not just the aforementioned Hugh Trevor-Roper, Richard Little-john, Jimmy Carter, and Germaine Greer—saying: *He brought this on himself, he got himself into trouble with "his own people" and now we have to get him out of it, he criticized Mrs. Thatcher but now her government is paying to save his neck and he's fine with that, and is there really anybody trying to kill him or does he just like the attention? And why are we paying all this money to protect him when he seems to be doing just fine? And we don't really like him anyway, because he's not a very nice man.*

(For the record: there were, to my knowledge, at least six assassination plots against me in the years after the fatwa, foiled by the expertise of the British intelligence services.)

Even more hurtful was the rejection by the people about whom I had written—had done so with, I thought, love. I could come to terms with the attack from Iran. It was a brutal regime, and I had nothing to do with it, except that it was trying to kill me. The hostility emanating from India and Pakistan and from South Asian communities in the United Kingdom was much harder to bear. That wound remains unhealed to this day. I have to accept that rejection, but it's hard. I entered another downward spiral during those years, and it was a while before I found my feet and began to find the language with which to fight back, and embarked upon the defense of free-speech principles, a much larger subject than the defense of my own work, which has become an important part of my life. If the hostility toward me continued, so be it. I made my home in literature and the imagination and did the best work I could.

As to safety: the years passed, and I understood that if I waited until somebody said to me, "Everything's fine now, you're safe," then that day would never come. The only person who could make the decision to emerge from the safety net of twenty-four-hour police protection and begin to lead a normal life once again was me.

I made the decision. Moving to New York in the year 2000 was an integral part of it, because in America there was no governmental authority insisting on keeping me inside the fist of the security forces. I could make my own choices. But this, the second transcontinental migration of my life, had its own problems.

———

The third rehab.

To remake a life of freedom—to be rehabilitated out of the maximum-security world and reintroduced into polite society—I had to overcome the fear that my mere presence was capable of inducing in others. Andrew Wylie invited me to stay with him and his wife, Camie, at their house in Water Mill, Long Island, to celebrate my move to the United States, and one night they took me out to dinner at the fashionable East Hampton restaurant Nick & Toni's, where I had never been. Soon after we were seated, the artist Eric Fischl passed by and paused to greet Andrew. Then he gestured in my direction. "Shouldn't we all be afraid and leave the restaurant?" he asked me. I tried to remain calm. "Well," I said, "I'm having dinner. You must do as you please."

I learned a lesson from this brief encounter. The only way I could stop looking, to others, like some sort of walking bomb was to behave, frequently and in public, as if there was nothing to be frightened of. Only by advertising my own lack of fear could I gradually persuade others not to be scared when I showed up. This wasn't easy. The *New York Post* put me on the front page, and ran a cartoon inside suggesting that I might be killed in New York. An American friend living in London wrote to me and said that if I didn't hire security immediately then "what we all feared" would happen soon. Milan was almost four years old, and his mother, Elizabeth, was reluctant to allow him to come and stay with me. And I had no way of being certain that there was nothing to be afraid of. I had only my instincts, and they said, *Live. Live.*

So I did. I embarked on a deliberate program of high-visibility outings where I would be photographed and my presence would probably be reported in the press. And it worked. People got used to the idea that I was around, living my life, and it wasn't causing anyone any problems. I achieved freedom by living like a free man. I became acceptable.

I didn't act on instinct alone. I met with officers of the New York City Police Department at the offices of the Wylie Agency, and they reassured me that they knew of no threats against me in the New York area. "The *Post* actually helped," one officer said. "Because if that kind of publicity didn't stir up any trouble, then that was useful information. And after it appeared, nothing happened. On all the channels that we monitor, there was zero interest." That was a reassuring thing to hear.

There was an unexpected and unfortunate side effect of my re-entry strategy. Maybe because the news media found my re-appearance shocking after a decade of near-invisibility, and because for the tabloid media—actually, not only the tabloid media—it had become a well-established practice to portray anything I said or did in a negative light, I was branded, almost overnight, as a shallow, frivolous, unserious, celebrity-craving "party animal." There was little or no attempt to understand what it might be like to be me, and almost no pleasure that I finally felt able to emerge from the security cocoon. This "party animal" trope has proved to be depressingly long-lasting. After the events of August 12, even one of my closest friends succumbed to it, saying, in a television interview, that now that I couldn't go to cocktail parties I could finally focus on my writing. Something like that. He told me, when I protested, that he had been trying to make a joke. He conceded that it hadn't, as he put it, "landed well."

The question arises (I've been asked this quite a few times since the attack): Was I wrong to make this new, carefree life for myself? With hindsight, shouldn't I have been more cautious, less open, more aware of the danger lurking in the shadows? Did I construct a fool's paradise for myself and find out, two decades later, just how big a fool I had been? Had I, so to speak, made myself available for the knife?

In other words—as so many people had said all along—was it my own fault?

To be absolutely truthful, in those first, physically weak, low-spirited days in the trauma ward in Erie, it was a question I asked myself. But as I grew stronger in body and mind, it was an analysis I rejected emphatically. To regret what your life has been is the true folly, I told myself, because the person doing the regretting has been shaped by the life he subsequently regrets. There were probably exceptions to this principle, but very few of the people who ought to regret their lives—Donald Trump, Boris Johnson, Adolf Eichmann, Harvey Weinstein—ever do so. At any rate: whether the general principle held up or not, in the situation in which I found myself it held up for me. I had had close to twenty-three years in New York living a full, rich life. There were mistakes along the way, plenty of those, and things I could have done better, and I do regret those, but my life in general? I'm glad I have lived it, and I've tried to live it as well as possible.

———

Post-traumatic stress disorder can manifest itself in a wide variety of ways: endless mental replays of the traumatic event, sudden panic attacks, depression. I didn't have those symptoms. What I had—what, as I write this, I still have several times a week—were and are nightmares.

When I was awake in my room at Hamot I heard the moans and screams of my neighbors. What I didn't hear were my own nocturnal performances. But there were nightmares every night, and I was flinging myself around in my bed and shouting and crying, and it was just as well that the bed had guardrails on both sides or I would certainly have fallen out. Eliza, woken up by my noise, would come and hold my hand and wake me gently and tell me it was all right.

But it wasn't. In my waking hours I was trying to stay calm, collected, optimistic, determined. But when I slept all my defenses fell away, and the night horrors came for me. My waking self, with its effortful composure, was, in a sense, a lie. The wild night language of my dreams told the truth. "Night language" is a Joycean term, but I will not here attempt to reproduce the language of *Finnegans Wake,* James Joyce's mammoth effort to create on the page the syntax of our sleeping minds. Plainer descriptions of my dreams will have to suffice.

The dreams were not replays of the attacks, but they were predominantly violent. In them an "I" figure was being pursued or attacked by an enemy, usually armed with a spear or sword, like the enemy I had dreamed up just before leaving home to go to Chautauqua. Sometimes the location was an arena, sometimes a cage, sometimes open countryside or a city street. But I was always in flight, always pursued, and very often I lost my footing and then I was rolling left and right on the ground, trying to avoid my enemy's downward thrusts. At these times I was also thrashing about in bed.

Not all the dreams featured me as the central character. I dreamed the blinding of the Earl of Gloucester by the Duke of Cornwall in *King Lear.* To be precise, I dreamed my sixty-year-old memory of being taken as a fifteen-year-old schoolboy on a school outing to Stratford-upon-Avon to see the famous Peter Brook production of *Lear* for the Royal Shakespeare Company, starring Paul Scofield as the king, Diana Rigg as Cordelia, and, as the tragic Gloucester and the vicious Cornwall, John Lawrie and Tony Church. "Upon these eyes of thine I'll set my foot." "Give me some help! O cruel! O you gods!" "Out, vile jelly! Where is thy lustre now?" My young self had been horrified by the scene, and I never forgot it. I never dreamed that a version of Gloucester's misery would be visited upon me. But I was dreaming it now.

There was also a strange dream that looked like Géricault's great painting *The Raft of the Medusa* brought to life, except that the people on the raft were all Surrealists—Max Ernst, René Magritte, Salvador Dalí, Luis Buñuel, even Leonora Carrington—and they were all fighting savagely, trying to gouge out one another's eyes.

I dreamed of being trapped in a crowd of people with white ceramic faces.

I dreamed of being in a plane making a forced landing while the passengers screamed, "We're all going to die."

I dreamed of a walled city under siege, and of myself at the head of the cavalry, galloping to the rescue, but in the dream I knew that our ride was too late, and we would not be able to arrive in time to prevent the city from being sacked and burned.

I dreamed about the cheapness of human lives, which were being bought and sold in a street market for antique money—annas, pice; shillings, farthings.

I dreamed of returning to my beloved Bombay—not Mumbai—and kneeling to kiss the tarmac as I came down from the plane, but when I looked up there was a crowd shouting at me, *"Dafa ho."* Begone.

I dreamed about casual murders. And the murderer was me. And killing felt like joy. When I woke up I had Johnny Cash on the brain, "Folsom Prison Blues." *I shot a man in Reno, just to watch him die.*

———

I wasn't supposed to begin working on my left hand, or using it in any way, until the six-week mark. It was captured in its splint like a caged bird. Meanwhile, my occupational therapist, Rose, friendly, matter-of-fact, with the same name as my granddaughter, helped me to learn how to clean myself in the shower one-handed, how to live, at least temporarily, in a one-handed world. Also a one-eyed world. When you can't see what or who is coming at you from the right, you have to teach yourself to turn your whole head frequently, to look in that direction. And you have to try not to let this depress you. You have to get better at pouring water into a glass, trusting the brain to make the adjustments it needs to make to compensate for your loss.

Your breathing needs to be tested regularly—inhale, exhale—there are machines to test the strength of both. Can you get out of bed (once the alarm has been switched off) and walk? Can you walk to the door of your room and go outside? Can you walk around the whole ward floor and back again? Can you walk to the physical-therapy gym, where your smiling, somewhat glamorous physical therapist, Faye, will take over from Rose? Can you use the exercise bike? Now can you go faster? Now, if we increase the resistance, can you still do it? Ten minutes? Twenty? Can you walk across the gym going heel-to-toe? Can you walk backward? Sideways? Up those stairs? Down those stairs? Can you weave your way through the little maze Faye has constructed for you? Are you feeling dizzy? Are you okay? Can you see the objects she has placed around the gym, some low down, some high up, some at eye level? Can you pass the tests that determine whether you are considered safe to be released into the world?—Oh, you're still not very strong, are you, not very stable.—There, you see? You're doing much better.—This is good. Now do it all again.

You're very determined, Rose and Faye both told me. That's good. That will help.

Four hours a day of Rose and Faye were doing me good. I was getting stronger and better able to deal with the new problems of everyday life. And once the urine-blocking medication was stopped, I felt a surge of optimism. Normal service might shortly be resumed. And a bound galley of *Victory City* arrived. For me, the best moment of the whole process of book publication is this one, the moment when you hold your printed book in your hand for the first time, and you feel its reality, its life. Because of what had happened to me, the last page of *Victory City*, when its central character, the poet Pampa Kampana, celebrates the power of words to outlast empires, concluding with the sentence "Words are the only victors," was already being widely quoted. Eliza asked me to read the page for her camera. As I did so, a lump formed in my throat. I had to fight to hold back the tears.

At least I was still, or would soon be again, a writer who had written a book.

———

Eliza asked me to talk to her camera about *The Satanic Verses*.

When I started writing that book, it never occurred to me that I wasn't allowed to do it. I had these stories I wanted to tell and I was trying to work out how to tell them. That was all I was doing.

(Sometimes I think I belong to another age. I can remember being in the garden of our house as a child in the 1950s, listening to my parents and their friends laughing and joking as they discussed everything under the sun, from contemporary politics to the existence of God, without feeling any pressure to censor or dilute their opinions. I also remember being at the apartment of my favorite uncle, Hameed Butt, who sometimes wrote for the movies, and his dancer-actress wife, Uzra, who sometimes acted in them. I watched them playing cards with their artsy-*filmi* crowd, speaking in even more outrageous language about everything and nothing, and laughing even more uproariously than my parents' friends. These settings were where I learned the first lesson of free expression—that you must take it for granted.

If you are afraid of the consequences of what you say, then you are not free. When I was making *The Satanic Verses*, it never occurred to me to be afraid.)

In fact, for a while I thought it might not be one book, but three. One book about the village that walked into the sea, a second about the birth-of-a-religion stuff, and a third, longer book about South Asian immigrants in contemporary London. Then I was on a plane to go, I think, to a literary festival in Australia, and I understood that all the stories were episodes from the life of the Archangel Gabriel, and I saw that it was one book. And the main character would be named Gibreel Farishta. Gibreel, Gabriel, and Farishta, angel. That was it. I wasn't trying to offend or insult anyone. I was trying to write a novel.

Truthfully, I would be happy never to speak about *The Satanic Verses* again. My poor maligned book. Maybe one day it, and its maligned author, will both be free again.

I was much happier to think about my new book. My dear friend Martin Amis liked to say, "When you publish a book, you either get away with it, or you don't get away with it."

I hoped that on this occasion I might get away with it.

———

There were unconfirmed rumors that I had been transported to Manhattan from Erie by unknown means, and was now a patient at Rusk. For several days after I arrived, there was a media presence in the street outside the hospital. After Milan's third visit to me, as he was leaving, a car crawled along beside him and a man called his name. "Milan!" He kept walking, the car kept pace with him, and again the man called out, "Milan!" Milan had the presence of mind to make a right turn against the flow of traffic, which prevented the car from following him any farther. The man was never there again, but Milan was worried. However, he remained calm. He was in New York to help care for his dad, and that was all that mattered.

On the day of the attack there had been extremely aggressive photographers on the sidewalk outside our home, and Eliza had been held, jostled, and pushed as she tried to get to the car service, already distraught at the thought that she was racing to see her dying husband. After that experience she was unable to do as I suggested and simply ignore the paparazzi. The way she saw it, unknown strangers were stalking her. How could she be sure they had only cameras in their hands?

She was sleeping at home, but the shutterbugs weren't there at night. If she left early in the morning she could avoid them, but she had work to do, she was in the final stages of edits of *Promise*. Given what had happened in our lives, this wasn't easy work, to say the least. But she is a strong-willed woman, and she got it done. When she had to walk her dog, an elderly border terrier named Hero, she saw the photographers lurking. Sometimes they stayed in their cars (she knew their cars by now); sometimes they rolled down the windows and the snouts of their long lenses pointed at her. Sometimes they got out and took pictures. This intrusive ritual was repeated when she left home in the afternoon to go to Rusk. None of these photographs were ever published. She wasn't the person whose picture they wanted, but they harassed her for weeks anyway. There are aspects of press freedom that aren't easy to defend.

————

Milan wanted to talk about Trump. I didn't, really. But I did say, "If he is re-elected this country may become impossible to live in."

I saw his eyes light up. "You mean you might come back to England?" I saw, not for the first time, how much he wanted that, and that in the aftermath of the attack, and in the light of his very real fear of flying, he wanted it even more.

"I don't know," I said. "Brexit Britain is pretty awful too." But, I added, before the attack Eliza and I had been talking about spending more time in London because, after all, almost all my close family members lived there. However, now was not the time to discuss that, I told him. I just needed to get back on my feet. "Let's put that conversation on hold."

I am torn between London and New York. The fact is, I prefer living in New York, but the pull of family and of most of my oldest friends is very strong. I still can't answer Milan's question. Let's put that conversation on hold.

―――――

As the days lengthened into weeks, I was recovering. But it wasn't over yet. For one thing, there was the issue of my other eye, my one remaining eye.

In George Orwell's *Nineteen Eighty-Four,* when people are taken into Room 101 in the basement of the Ministry of Love, what they encounter in that fearsome torture chamber is— according to the evil O'Brien, agent of the Thought Police—"the worst thing in the world." The worst thing in the world is different for every individual. For Winston Smith, the novel's protagonist, the worst thing in the world is rats.

For me, it always was, and still is, blindness.

Many readers of *Victory City* have wondered if the scene in which the heroine is blinded was written, or rewritten, after the August 12 attack. Some have even found it hard to believe that it wasn't. But it wasn't. When I wrote that scene I was writing about a lifelong fear: "the worst thing in the world." And now my right eye was gone and the left suffered from macular degeneration, a condition of the retina which can lead to an almost complete loss of vision. And that was the only eye I had left.

The treatment I had been receiving, for several years, took the form of an injection directly into the white of the eye, every month or so. I received one such injection during my time at Rusk; after my release I would return to my regular eye specialist, who told me that I was responding exceptionally well to the medication, and so the condition was stable.

I can only hope that that continues to be the case. If not, I'll be locked into Room 101 for as long as I have left.

———

Also: My blood pressure was a worry. It was low, and when I stood up it often dropped lower, and there was dizziness, and I had to sit down. I said to one of the nurses who came to check my vital signs that I was surprised because I had never previously had any problems with blood pressure. She replied kindly, "You lost a lot of blood, you know."

I was asked to wear a corset, tightly held together by Velcro, to help prevent the sudden drops in pressure. That helped. On two occasions I was given blood transfusions. They helped, too. I was also put on a medication designed to boost my blood pressure, and that began to work. The readings were still low, but they were at the low end of the acceptable range. That didn't feel so bad.

———

As the weeks inched by at Rusk, I was running a little low on gumption. I was beginning to be irritated by little things—for instance, the time it took for a nurse to show up after I rang the bell for attention, which could be a real problem if I needed to go to the bathroom and couldn't get out of the bed by myself because it would begin to scream. (By this time, I felt stronger on my legs and was perfectly capable of walking to the toilet, but I was a prisoner of my bed.) I had been, I think, a good patient, but now I was impatient. I told Eliza, "We need to start talking about a release date."

We were given a tentative release date—Friday, September 23—which was exactly three weeks after I arrived at Rusk, exactly six weeks after the attack. But as the date approached, I was told they would rather delay it by a few days at least.

The head man—I'll call him Dr. O.—came to see me on his rounds to tell me this. The team had met to discuss my condition, and this delay was its collective view. But I had set my heart on the date, and the delay felt unbearable. I had an emotional explosion. I needed to go home, I said. This place was becoming bad for me. Everything was in pretty good order. My physical therapist, Faye, said I had passed the tests that allowed her to declare me fit to be released. My occupational therapist, Rose, also declared herself happy with my progress. The injuries seemed to have healed. The blood pressure was under control. Let me go.

"If you leave," Dr. O. said, gently, "it will be against medical advice."

"All right," I said, with much too much feeling in my voice. "I accept that."

That was, if memory serves, on Wednesday. On Thursday, I got out of bed (it had been silenced) and felt suddenly very dizzy indeed. I sat down fast. The doctors had been right and I had been wrong. I needed to stay until the blood pressure was really under control.

Meanwhile: Eliza and Sameen had been talking. They were worried about my returning home. If the paparazzi were watching the address, other people might also be watching, and those other people might be carrying things other than long-lensed cameras. It was Sameen who first told me that Eliza had another plan. Good friends had offered us the use of their loft in SoHo. They were in Los Angeles and wouldn't be back in New York until Thanksgiving and would love to be able to help. They would tell the doorman we would be there and give him a pseudonym which we would set with them. This would be totally private and therefore a better, safer way of re-entering the world. When Sameen told me this I reacted negatively. I just wanted to go home. I didn't want another way station. I wanted to sleep in my own bed, and to have my books around me. But when I saw that Eliza and Milan were united in their preference for the SoHo option, I relented. "Okay," I said, "let's go there."

Eliza had been meeting with professional security outfits. She told me which one she preferred, and we entered into a relationship with them. This would not be cheap, but, for the foreseeable future at least, it felt necessary. Our security would send a team to bring me away from Rusk when the time came, and they would liaise with the NYPD as well. I felt a little like a package being scheduled for delivery, but I accepted the rules.

On Monday, September 26, I was given the all-clear by the Rusk medical team. Rehab was over. After more than six weeks in two hospitals, I could return to the world.

PART TWO

The Angel of Life

5

Homecoming

The plan was to leave Rusk at 3 a.m., as quietly as possible, and get down to Mercer Street through the empty night-city to avoid any watching eyes. I was packed and ready by 1:00 and Eliza arrived an hour later, accompanied, for moral support, by our dear friend Suphala, tabla player extraordinaire. We embraced happily. Eliza was very stressed but trying not to show it, because I was highly excited. (I saw her tension anyway.) We were given an envelope containing my discharge papers, a timetable of medications, a few bottles of pills (painkillers if needed, Lipitor, and something to boost my blood pressure), an asthma inhaler, and some antibiotic eye ointment. I put on my Velcro corset to make sure I could walk without feeling light-headed. Then one of our security team was outside the door along with an NYPD officer, and the exit began. On the day before, I had been taken downstairs to see the side door we would be using, to familiarize myself with the route and make sure I could manage the few steps down to the street level. *I came in here on a stretcher and I'm leaving on my own two feet,* I thought, allowing myself a moment of self-congratulation. A large black Escalade SUV was waiting with its motor running. It wasn't easy to climb up into it, because of my one-handedness, but I managed to do it unaided. Eliza and Suphala got in too, and we were off.

I had never felt such exhilaration while driving through Manhattan. I remembered a similar feeling when I was taking a yellow cab home on June 29, 2016, just after I had been sworn in as an American citizen. That afternoon the city had suddenly felt different, as if it now belonged to me, or I to it. That had been a powerful feeling. This was even bigger, and I made myself a promise while we floated through the New York night: *I'm going to take back as much of my life here as possible, as soon as I possibly can.*

We entered the building on Mercer, and the night doorman gave us a nod of welcome with no sign of recognition. Up we went, and as we entered our friends' beautiful apartment I thought, *I'm free. I'm alive, and I'm free.* It was 3:30 A.M., and I found my way to a large, comfortable, and definitely non-screaming bed. I got into it and Eliza lay down next to me and then, suddenly, she was sobbing uncontrollably as all the stress poured out of her.

"My husband's home," she sobbed. "My husband's home."

———

There are moments, such as this, when these events are painful to set down.

———

We had been able to sleep luxuriously late, uninterrupted by 4 A.M. bloodletters or 5 A.M. nurses or 6 A.M. doctors. During hospital nights, darkness is an intermittent grace, and your bed is not your friend, so the comfort of the Mercer Street bed and the curtained darkness of the room were soothing novelties. We didn't want to start the day. When we finally did get up and draw back the curtains, the city stretched out before us like a gift. The loft had windows on three sides, so we could look downtown toward the soaring One World Trade building, or westward across the Village to the Hudson River, or north past the New York University faculty residential towers on Bleecker Street all the way to the Empire State Building. There was a roof terrace on which our hosts had planted a gorgeous garden in the sky. If this wasn't home, it was the next best thing. It felt like a vacation.

We weren't entirely alone for the first few days. Eliza had wanted some trained support in case things didn't go smoothly with me, and she hired a twenty-four-hour nursing service, a night nurse and a day nurse, to be with us. Happily, we soon agreed that this wasn't necessary. Just being out of the hospital felt like a cure. I was stronger every day.

Peace and quiet and the illusion of a return to private life lasted two days. Then the medical world reached out and grabbed me, and told me I still had a long way to go. More precisely: my hand therapist, Monica, visited for the first time. She was small, Chinese American, smiling, friendly, a book lover and big reader, and utterly ruthless when it came to getting my hand moving again.

"This is going to hurt."

"Ow!"

"This is going to hurt even more."

She was scheduled to visit three times a week. The first thing she did, on that first visit, was cut off the splint. "You don't need this anymore." My left hand immediately felt unshackled, even though, as Milan afterward told me, "you really couldn't move your fingers at all, Dad." Monica told me the tendons had healed.

I was past the six-week mark, and now, she told me, it was time to exercise and use the hand as much as possible; which was easy to say but not easy to do when it was all but immobile.

The tendons run in channels inside the hand, and now that they were in one piece again, they needed to relearn how to move up and down in those channels. I had thought, innocently, that physical therapy would do the trick in a few months. I now learned that it wasn't necessarily as straightforward as that. There was a real chance that, instead of the tendons' beginning to glide smoothly in their channels and allowing my hand to resume business as usual, clenching and unclenching and so forth, there was another, unpleasant possibility: instead of loosening up, they might adhere to their channels and be stuck in one position, in which case more major surgery would be required to try and unstick them. Hearing that made my heart sink, but it also provided very strong motivation to put everything into the repair work. If it was going to hurt, so be it. I wanted my hand back.

Monica's first business was to attend to the dried blood which was disfiguring my palm, and also making it harder for things to start moving. She chipped away at it every time she came. She had a variety of tools that she used during her visits. They looked like strange bluish-green, translucent sea monsters and acted like instruments of torture. She also gave me exercises to do in her absence and a whirring tool to apply to the scar tissue.

"I can't do it as hard as you can," I said.

"I know," she said. "It's hard to cause yourself pain."

The story of my hand would stretch over the next six months. As well as my sessions with Monica, I had appointments, every six weeks or so, with a hand surgeon at NYU Langone, Dr. Y. At our first meeting he wasn't exactly cheering. He told me plainly, "In the case of an injury as severe as yours we usually don't have a very optimistic prognosis."

There was the question of movement, and then there was the question of feeling. As to movement, at the beginning there was very little. As to feeling, I had some in my thumb and index finger, none in the middle finger and ring finger, a small amount in the little finger. The palm of my hand between the scar and the wrist had feeling; above the scar, there was none. Dr. Y. could not tell me how much feeling, if any, might return. He hoped Monica's work would restore a degree of movement at least. "For the rest, we can hope."

I left Dr. Y.'s consulting room determined to prove him wrong. "Go for it, Monica," I told her at our next session.

"This is going to hurt," she said.

"Ow."

Let me accelerate into the future. With much exercise, the joints of my fingers started bending again. The target we had before us was that I should be able to make a fist. The first step was to be able to touch my fingertips to my palm. On the day I did that, I wanted to cheer. Then, slowly, I began to be able to curl the fingers inward. The fist was definitely getting closer.

I also had to reach my thumb across my hand and touch the tip of my little finger. (You will have noticed that I resist using the American "pinkie"/"pinky.") For a long time that felt like a journey across interstellar space. And then—lo!—the day came when it wasn't. Thumb, little finger, please meet. I'm pretty sure you guys have met before.

Once a month, Monica monitored my progress. On March 8, 2023, just under seven months after the knife entered the palm of my hand, the results were good. The blood was gone from the wound, the long scar had softened and was no longer impeding the movement of the thumb, the thumbs-up on the left hand was identical to the right hand, the fist was just about as good as the right fist, the fingers could move independently of one another, and, thanks to a lot of work with putty, the strength of the hand had begun to increase. Still not good enough, but better. As for feeling, it wasn't a whole lot better. The thumb and index finger were fine; the little finger had improved feeling; the other two—not so much. But what was called "protective feeling" had returned even to those fingers. I could feel heat, so I wouldn't burn myself, and I could feel sharpness, so I wouldn't cut myself. These were always the first feelings that returned, I was told. How intelligent the human body was, I thought, admiringly. What a wonder it is, this thing we all inhabit. *What a piece of work is a man.*

The following week, I went back to see Dr. Y. and showed off my new skills. He said the thing every patient wants to hear: "The recovery of your hand is miraculous." Miraculous! Yes! Yes, it is! "The feeling may take another six months to return, and you just have to wait, because the nerves . . ." The nerves are slow! I know about the slow nerves! That's okay! "In fact, it may be a year before you know how much feeling you'll get back. Can you type?" Yes. I can type. I can tie shoelaces and uncork wine bottles and turn doorknobs and hold a full glass of water. I'm almost a human being.

"You don't have to come back and see me anymore," Dr. Y. said. "And you don't need to see Monica anymore either."

I felt a little sad. Monica and I got on very well. And she had declared her intention to read all my books in chronological order. She had finished *Grimus* and was most of the way through *Midnight's Children.* "You have a long road ahead," I told her.

"I'm going to do it," she said. "I'm discovering that you write very well." And with a hug she was gone; and I had a moving hand again.

Rewind.

I might have left the hospital in late September 2022, but hospitals hadn't left me. Beginning the week after Monica started work on my hand, there followed three months of outpatient appointments with specialists in various different regions of my anatomy, by whom I was examined, often in intimate detail. By the end of this long sequence of encounters, I knew the NYU Langone hospital network better than I had ever expected to. And it, in its turn, knew just about everything about me and my insides.

(We were concerned about security, and on all these visits I was accompanied by members of the team we had hired. It was very helpful that we could live anonymously in the SoHo loft, so that my comings and goings could take place out of the public eye.)

The first appointment was with a urologist. Dr. U. needed to check whether the urination problem I'd had at Rusk had gone away. I confirmed that it had. He wanted a blood sample. He wanted a urine sample. I obediently provided both. Then he asked when I had last had my prostate gland examined. It had been a while, I told him. "I'll just take a look," he said.

Oh, well, okay, then, why not. I'm here because of a knife attack, but let's check the prostate, sure. Bend over, spread your legs, lubricant, rubber gloves, aaagh. That's uncomfortable. Now it's even more uncomfortable. No, don't hurry, take your time. And . . . it's done.

After the examination, a nasty surprise. "I felt something," said Dr. U. "It's small. A small bump on the prostate. We should check it out. I'll order a quick MRI scan." I was at a loss for words. Really? After I narrowly survived a murder attempt, now I had to face the prospect of cancer? This was unacceptable. It was *unfair.*

"It's probably nothing," said Dr. U.

Fast-forward again. A week after my appointment with Dr. U., I had my MRI scan, as well as an ultrasound on my right leg, which was deemed to be a little thicker than the left, and the ultrasound was to check if there were any blood clots in it. On the way home, I looked in Langone's MyChart app. The results were posted quickly. There was good news and bad news. The good news was: no blood clots; my leg was fine. The bad news was mostly expressed in incomprehensible medicalese but contained, as if in neon letters, the clear, regular-English words *cancer likely*. On the 1-to-5 scale of probability they used, I had scored a wretched 4.

Cancer likely.

A phone call with Dr. U. He had seen the report, but there was something he was puzzled by. The normal test for prostate cancer is a PSA, a blood test that measures the amount of prostate-specific antigen in your blood. A high PSA number is considered dangerous, a low number is reassuring. The PSA number on my blood test was low: 2.1. This would normally be read to mean "no prostate problem." But the MRI result said *cancer likely*. The results were contradictory. Dr. U. was asking for a second opinion from the head of urology, who would be in touch with me. When I had my video conference with him, this gentleman—Dr. U-2—turned out to be Indian American, and a bit of a fan. He was also very smart. "When you were at Rusk," he said, "you had a urinary difficulty, including a UTI." Yes, I said, quite a bad urinary-tract infection, and I had only just stopped taking the antibiotics.

He said that he thought the UTI might be responsible for the bump on my prostate. "It can cause inflammation," he said. "I think the MRI was taken too soon. We have to wait some weeks and then do another one." So, then, I probably didn't have can-

cer? Cancer unlikely? He was noncommittal: we should wait for
the results, he said. Later, I talked to my therapist, who was
more reassuring. "If the PSA is that low, then this senior urologist is probably right, this is an inflammation caused by the UTI."
Anyway, he further reassured me, even if it was cancer, prostate
cancer was treatable, and I shouldn't worry about the delay before the second MRI. "It spreads very slowly." So I was left dan-
gling.

Things moved with glacial slowness. Three weeks later, I had
an in-person appointment with Dr. U-2, and here we go again, I
thought, bend over, spread your legs, lubricant, rubber gloves,
aaagh. Double aaagh. Even more aaagh. And . . . it's done.

"I feel nothing," Dr. U-2 said.

"Really? No bump? Nothing?"

"Nothing."

"That's good news, right? No bump means no cancer?"

"It's good news."

"So it was inflammation caused by the UTI?"

"I believe so."

"And now we can forget about it?"

"Well," said Dr. U-2, dampening my spirits, "we should wait a
few weeks more and then do another MRI scan. If that's clear,
then perhaps I don't need to do a needle biopsy."

A needle biopsy involved putting my legs up in stirrups, wide
apart. The needle went in through the perineum. It took about
ten minutes. It would be very unpleasant.

"I hope you don't," I said, weakly.

I had told hardly anyone about the prostate scare. It wasn't
cancer yet, I reasoned, and the C-word would induce panic in
the family. No need for them to panic until there was something
to panic about. I told Eliza. But otherwise I kept it to myself.

The second MRI took place in December, five weeks after

Dr. U-2's inspection, two months after the message reading *cancer likely*. This time the scan was clear. On the scale of 1 to 5, I was now a proud 1. There was no lump. I didn't have prostate cancer. The universe was not quite as cruel as that, even though it had waited two long months to tell me so. Now I told Sameen. She was furious with me for not having told her before.

———

Back in October, one week after we moved to SoHo, Milan and Eliza had both tested positive for Covid. I remained negative, but neither of them could be around me. For a week, I relied on friends to ferry in food and supplies to me. And the good news / bad news cycle continued. The morning after Milan's and Eliza's positive tests, I had an appointment with an ear, nose, and throat specialist to check out the progress of the deep wounds around my neck. (I thought of him as Dr. ENT, as if he were an ancient tree-creature from *The Lord of the Rings*.) "Good news," said Dr. ENT. "Everything looks good. It has all healed well." That day, I was able to shave (carefully) for the first time in seven and a half weeks. That felt terrific, a real positive step. But the same afternoon, I visited a cardiologist. Dr. Heart wanted another scan of the area under my right lung. The scan revealed that the fluid I'd had drained at Erie had reappeared. At eight the next morning, I had a surgical procedure to drain it again. This time there was even more than the first time: over a thousand cc's. My protein levels were very low, the result of the serious blood loss, and I was told that this was the likely cause of the accumulating fluid. I was put on a high-protein diet and told to come back in a couple of months for another scan. "If the fluid returns," Dr. Heart told me, "we may have to think again." That sounded menacing.

Eliza tested negative after five days, and I was hugely relieved when she returned to Mercer Street. Milan went on testing positive for another five days after that. Before he returned, I had some very good news.

———

The appointment I had been dreading the most was the one about my eye. It took place on October 10, the same day as the first MRI scan, the one that suggested I might have prostate cancer, so I wasn't feeling in great shape. The noted eye specialist Dr. Irina Belinsky had come to visit me at Rusk, when my right eye was still swollen, even behind its sewn-down eyelid. (I'm using her real name because she was so emotionally important to me in dealing with this, the worst of my wounds; no Dr. Eye for her.) "We have to wait until the swelling is down," she had told me then, "before we can make choices about how to proceed." I was genuinely afraid of what those choices might be. I asked Eliza to come with me to the appointment. I needed someone to hold my hand.

Dr. Belinsky inspected the eye. "The swelling has gone down," she said. "The eyelid can close by itself now. So, if you like, I can cut the stitches right away."

"Will it hurt?" I asked, like a baby. "And I hope you don't have to redo the stitches later, because that was very painful indeed."

"You don't need them anymore," she said. "Don't worry."

The cutting of the stitches didn't take long, and the eye felt better immediately, more naturally at rest.

"So now you have three options," Dr. Belinsky said. "There are three ways in which you could go forward.

"Option one is we do nothing. If the eye is peaceful, there's no irritation, no discomfort, just leave it as it is.

"Option two, we can make for you a ceramic eye. This will be made to a very high standard to match the exact coloring of your other eye, and it will fit over the damaged eye. It's very realistic. Some people like this a lot, others find it uncomfortable.

"Option three is to remove the eye. After that it will take approximately six weeks for the socket to heal. Then you can be fitted with a prosthetic, a false eye. Obviously, this is the most radical option."

I was grateful for her clarity, and immediately knew the direction I preferred. "I have never been able to use contact lenses," I told her. "I'm squeamish about putting things onto my eyes and taking them out, doing that every day. So I think the ceramic eye wouldn't work for me. And option three . . . To be frank, after all the surgery I've been through, I'm not attracted to the prospect of more. So, if there's a way of dealing with the eye that doesn't involve surgery, I'll take that. I'll go for option one. We do nothing."

"I just want to be sure that the eye feels comfortable," Dr. Belinsky said. "You'll need to go on putting the erythromycin ointment into it every day."

"It's comfortable," I said. "And, yes, using the ointment is fine."

"Good," she said. "And remember that this is not a forever decision. If, in one year, two years, five years, the eye begins to feel irritated, come back, and at that time, if such a time comes, we can make a different choice."

I felt a huge flood of relief. I had had nightmares about my eye being pulled out of my head, dreams reminiscent of *Un Chien Andalou*, the Surrealist film by Luis Buñuel and Salvador Dalí, in which a cloud slicing across the full moon becomes a razor blade slicing through an eye. *Do nothing* felt wonderful. Eliza saw the tension lift from my brow and squeezed my hand. "Okay, baby," she said. "We'll do that."

Two days later, I had to have the next installment of the injection in my left eye to treat the macular degeneration. "Look after this eye, doc," I said. "It's all I've got."

And that, for now at any rate, is the story of my eye(s).

Our world began to feel a little less isolated. Milan escaped Covid jail and we hung out again. Eliza felt able to leave us together watching Baz Luhrmann's *Elvis* while she went to a friend's birthday party. The governor of New York, Kathy Hochul, called to offer sympathy and solidarity, which was nice of her. Some of my oldest and closest friends came to visit us, including several who came all the way from London. All of them professed amazement at my good health. I told none of them about the bumps in the road (or on my prostate).

We watched a live stream of an event in my support at the British Library in London. By now there had been such events in Toronto and Denmark as well as the first event, at the New York Public Library. I joked to Milan that all these occasions had something of the feeling of memorial celebrations. "When I actually do die, nothing will happen, because it's all already been done." Milan didn't think it was a funny joke, so I didn't tell him that it also reminded me a bit of an anecdote in Bertrand Russell's autobiography. He had been hospitalized during a visit to China, and by the time the news got back to England it had been somewhat exaggerated and reports were published of his death; whereupon all the papers published his obituaries, and these were brought to him in his Chinese hospital bed, so he could read them.

Of course, I was moved and made happy by all the love and support. And I was also happy to be passing some of my medical tests. General Surgery, for example, declared that all the stab wounds in my chest and abdomen had healed. That was good to hear. But there were more bumps in the road ahead.

We come to the story of my mouth.

One of the wounds in my neck had cut a nerve and caused a partial paralysis of the right side of my lower lip. This, I was told, was irreversible. It had the visual effect of making my mouth slide over to the left when I spoke, and created the practical problem of causing me to bite my lip when I ate. And there were other problems. My mouth had stopped opening properly; it opened approximately half as wide as it had before the attack. This meant it was harder to eat. Fortunately, I didn't have any problems swallowing, but food had to be cut up into small pieces. I couldn't put a sandwich in my mouth. There was tightness at the corners, and a few strange side effects. If I put anything cold in there, I felt a line of coldness going down from the left corner of the mouth toward the jaw, as if something were leaking out. But nothing was. This was simply the new mouth I had to learn to live with. There was no cure.

I was sent to see a woman who worked with cancer patients but was reputed to know a wide range of mouth exercises. I went. There were exercises. I learned to do them. I still do them. They don't really help. She recommended I go to see an eminent dental surgeon who might be able to build something I could slip into my mouth to push the lower lip out a little, to prevent me from biting it. At the end of October, I went to see the eminent dental surgeon. He built me what I suppose one should call a prosthesis, a gizmo that clips over the teeth on the right side and does indeed push the lower lip out, and when I wear it the mouth looks a little more normal and it's easier to eat.

All of this took many weeks. After the prosthesis was made and fitted—in late November—it took me a while to get used to it, but then it began to feel natural, and I didn't even notice it was there. That was all very good. The nasty surprise was the bill. It turned out that neither the eminent dental surgeon nor the device itself was covered by my insurance. Nobody had told me this, which his assistant afterward acknowledged was a mistake. If I had been told, I would probably have decided to do without the prosthesis.

The bill, which did not include the eminent dental surgeon's fees, was for eighteen thousand dollars.

———

Eight weeks after his arrival in New York, Milan sailed home, on October 25. I had loved having him with me for such a long stretch. Feeling his love had helped me find my equilibrium again. Once he was gone, I began to feel restless in our beautiful temporary accommodation. I wanted my own bedroom, my own familiar environment. The news frenzy around me had calmed down; the paparazzi were getting bored and often not on our block. It was time to return.

Milan went ashore in Southampton on November 1, and took a train back to London. Three days later, it was my turn to travel—a shorter distance, but one of profound emotional significance. I was going home.

In Kenneth Grahame's classic children's book *The Wind in the Willows*, Mole, who has wandered away from his mole hole to start "messing about in boats" on the river with his friend the Water Rat, and worrying about the mischievous and irrepressible Mr. Toad of Toad Hall, is plodding along one night with Ratty through what he believes to be "strange country" when all of a sudden he is captivated by a scent:

> It was one of these mysterious fairy calls from out the void that suddenly reached Mole in the darkness, making him tingle through and through . . .
>
> Home! That was what they meant, those caressing appeals, those soft touches wafted through the air, those invisible little hands pulling and tugging, all one way!

And when he has followed the scent and found his old home, and after a pleasant supper is settling down for the night in his own bed, he muses:

He saw clearly how plain and simple . . . it all was; but clearly, too, how much it all meant to him, and the special value of some such anchorage in one's existence . . . this place which was all his own, these things which were so glad to see him again and could always be counted upon for the same simple welcome.

Home. *Dulce Domum*, Kenneth Grahame calls it, Sweet Home. It was twelve weeks to the day since the attack that had made it impossible to return here. Now, as my front door closed behind me, I was that humble Mole, recognizing the smells of the place, my heart leaping as I saw the photograph of myself and my sisters reading *Peter Pan* that hung above the fireplace, feeling the welcome of my bookshelves, the familiarity of my workspace, and finally the mothering kindness of my own bed enveloping me, folding its arms around me, hugging me into a deep and carefree sleep. I felt 100 percent better and healthier immediately. I was home.

———

We began to take very small steps back toward ordinary life. We had a few evenings at the homes of friends. At one of the earliest of these, at Alba and Francesco Clemente's place, Fran Lebowitz, who does not beat about the bush, had questions for me. "You're right-handed, correct?" she asked. "Then why did you put up your left hand to defend yourself?"

"I don't know, Fran," I said. "I wasn't really thinking about it." Then I thought about it. "Maybe it's a boxing thing," I offered.

"If you're a right-handed boxer you defend with your left and punch with your right, right?"

Fran was unimpressed. "Salman, two things," she said. "In the first place, you're not a boxer. And in the second place, you weren't punching him."

This is true, Fran, I conceded. Both in the first place and in the second place. I was not the puncher. I was the punchee.

Later, Francesco told me that Fran had been very concerned about me after the attack. "I think about him every day," she had said. This brought a smile to my face. "I want that on a T-shirt," I said. "'Fran Lebowitz thinks about me every day.'"

It was exciting to be doing something as "normal" as going to visit friends. But it could be very emotional too. We visited the Brooklyn home of the Grove Atlantic publisher, Morgan Entrekin, and his wife, the photographer Rachel Cobb. The evening was unforgettable, because the other guests at the table were Martin Amis and his wife, Isabel Fonseca. Martin had been fighting esophageal cancer for the past two years—the same cancer that had killed his closest friend, Christopher Hitchens. He had chemotherapy, it worked, he was in remission, then the tumor returned, he had more chemotherapy, it didn't work, and then he had surgery, and was told it had been successful. When we saw him at Morgan and Rachel's, he was painfully thin and his voice was faint, but his intelligence was undimmed and he was warm and loving toward me. We had both almost died, he said, so we were brothers in arms against death.

Soon afterward we were invited to Martin and Isabel's place at the top of a Brooklyn tower. James Fenton and Darryl Pinckney were there too. It was the last time I saw Martin. After that, his cancer took an unbreakable hold, and he was lost to us all.

On that second evening, he seemed even more frail, even skinnier, his voice even more diminished. But at that time the cancer had not returned, or we were not told that it had. It reappeared a few weeks later, however, and Isabel told me, "There is no hope of recovery." She said he was being calm as he faced the end, saying, "I've had a very good life." She sounded devastated. They had been together for thirty years.

There have been many times since the attack when I have thought that Death was hovering over the wrong people. Wasn't I the one earmarked for collection by the Reaper, the one about whom everyone agreed that the odds were strongly against my surviving? And yet here I was, upright, well established in the recovery room, and turning back toward Life, while around me some of my closest friends were falling over. Bill Buford— former editor of *Granta* magazine, former fiction editor of *The New Yorker*, author of one book about British football (soccer) hooligans (*Among the Thugs*) and two books about, respectively, Italian and French food (*Heat, Dirt*), a man who had eaten too much rich food in his life and had long-term issues with his heart—passed out on a city sidewalk and actually briefly died. He was saved by a man who saw him fall, ran into his building, and came out with a defibrillator. What were the odds against that? And on the day after Christmas, my younger-brother-in-literature Hanif Kureishi passed out in Rome and when he regained consciousness he couldn't move his arms or his legs. He has been writing—or, rather, dictating—a beautifully brave, honest, and funny blog on Substack about his travails, and there is some improvement in his mobility, but at present it's unclear when (or if) he will regain the use of his right, writing hand. And four days after I heard about Hanif, I learned that Paul Auster had lung cancer. Paul and his wife, Siri Hustvedt, had both participated in the event supporting me on the steps of the library, but now they were facing a crisis of their own. Paul had a chance of beating the cancer, he told me on the phone. One tumor, in one lung, not metastasized, not in the lymph nodes or anywhere else in his body, and he hoped the chemotherapy and immuno-therapy could reduce its size drastically, and then the infected section of his lung could be surgically removed. So: fingers crossed.

And Martin was dying. He didn't want to see friends, Isabel said. He saw James Fenton once, but that was it. He went down with Isabel to their house in Palm Beach so he could be warm and sit in the garden and read. He had said he was writing a story. He may or may not have finished it. His children came to see him. He was hardly eating. The angel was very close.

Isabel said that because of the tumor it was hard for him to speak on the phone but he liked getting emails. I wrote to him, "sending," I said, "a friendly wave in your direction." Martin had never been a great emailer, so I was surprised to receive a lengthy answer. It was so laudatory that I can't reproduce it all, but he did say this:

> When we recently saw each other for the first time since the atrocity, I have to admit that I expected you to be altered, di-minished in some way. Not a bit of it: you were and are intact and entire. And I thought with amazement, He's EQUAL to it.

Which may not be true, but it was kind. I wrote back at greater length. I give it here in full, because it felt to me then, and feels to me now, like saying goodbye.

My dear Martin

In response to your plunge towards length I'll try and ex-ceed the Twitter allowance too.

In the first place I have to tell you how moved I am by the generosity and kindness of your words. No writer could wish for a better verbal embrace.

In the second place I want to say about your writing that it is characterized by both brilliance and fearlessness—by brilliance I mean not only linguistic brilliance, though you have certainly always had that, but formal inventiveness, comic pyrotechnics, and high intelligence; and under "fearlessness" I group your willingness (no, your need) to take on the central material of your times, political, moral, sexual, all of it.

This body of work has transformed and energized English literature and has inspired and will go on inspiring those who come after us. You have taken the baton passed by Bellow, Nabokov and your father and you will pass it on to . . . I don't know who . . . someone with the talent and wisdom to grab it and run with it.

So, bravo, bravo, dear friend.

What you have made will long endure.

With admiration and love,

Salman.

In those sad last days I often found myself remembering the times, over thirty years ago now, when Martin would organize poker nights. One characteristic of these evenings was that one never found out anything about the other players' lives. If the conversation strayed toward the personal, or the political, someone would immediately cry, "Play poker!"—whereupon we dutifully returned our attention to the important things.

I remembered, too, that before I moved to New York, before

Ian McEwan and his wife, Annalena McAfee, bought their mansion in the Cotswold countryside, before Martin and Isabel showed up in Brooklyn, the three of us—Martin, Ian, and I—used to have fairly frequent meals together, usually at Elena's L'Étoile on Charlotte Street in London, to set the world to rights. A Sunday newspaper had published a montage of the three of us under some such headline as "The Godfathers," and we had agreed that, as the heads of the crime families that made up literary London, we should meet regularly to make sure all things were arranged well and no unnecessary shooting wars began.

It is the trivia of the past that one mourns as much as greater matters (such as literary talent) when one is saying goodbye to a friend.

One of the reasons Alfred Hitchcock's film *Psycho* is so frightening is that the wrong people die. The biggest star in the movie, Janet Leigh, is dead after only half an hour or so. The safe, avuncular, leave-it-to-me detective Martin Balsam shows up, and the next thing we know he's dead too. It's terrifying. That was how I was beginning to feel. Death was showing up at the wrong addresses.

We were all getting older. *There isn't going to be less of this, is there?* I thought. Angela Carter, Bruce Chatwin, Raymond Carver, Christopher Hitchens had all left early. Now an entire generation was nearing the exits.

Martin died in his sleep, peacefully and without pain, on the night of May 19, 2023.

At the Rushdie-Griffiths residence, however, the mood barometer had been swinging upward ever since December. The

World Cup was on TV, and I watched almost every game. Lionel Messi's Argentina became world champions, which pleased me. Closer to home, the news was getting better in many ways. (Not the real news, which was full of insane gun violence and equally insane Trump and Trumpublicans, as usual.) Eliza's *Promise* got good British publishers, and they would publish in early July, almost simultaneously with the United States. As for me, I felt stronger every day. And then, on December 2 and 5, I faced the two final medical hurdles, and cleared them both. The X-ray looking at my lungs came back clear. The protein diet had worked! The fluid had not returned! *Check*. And three days later: the second MRI scan gave me the all-clear on the prostate! I didn't have to fear either the needle biopsy or the cancer (I wasn't sure which scared me more). *Big check*. I had no more medical issues to resolve. I emerged from the long tunnel of hospital visits and was returned to the general population.

It was Eliza's birthday on December 6. Suphala and Kiran Desai came over, and we ordered in a feast from a nearby restaurant. We had much to celebrate.

For example: I no longer had to worry about being overweight. As the screaming bed at Rusk (which could also weigh me) had informed me, I had lost fifty-five pounds. I had spent months living first in hospital gowns and then in sweatpants and T-shirts, but now that I could try on my clothes at home I found that all the trousers I owned literally fell off me. I was pleased about the weight loss (though I agreed with everyone that it was not a diet plan to be recommended), and pleasantly surprised by some side effects (my asthma was much improved, and I no longer snored, to the relief of the other person in the bed), but the clothes situation was a problem, even if it was true that the quality of my problems was improving. Trousers falling down were funny. Knife attacks were not.

I was suffering somewhat from euphoria, declaring myself well, our troubles over, and announcing that our happy future ought immediately to begin. One of the biggest reasons for such overconfidence was that I was able to sit at my desk again and feel the juices beginning to flow. For three months I hadn't been able to think about writing. When I finally did, and I looked into the notes I'd been making for a possible novel to follow *Victory City*, it felt absurd. *I can't write this,* I told myself. However much I wanted to focus on fiction, something immense and non-fictional had happened to me, and I saw that Andrew Wylie had been right. Until I dealt with the attack, I wouldn't be able to write anything else. I understood that I had to write the book you're reading now before I could move on to anything else. To write would be my way of owning what had happened, taking charge of it, making it mine, refusing to be a mere victim. I would answer violence with art.

I don't like to think of writing as therapy—writing is writing, and therapy is therapy—but there was a good chance that telling the story as I saw it might make me feel better.

There were some lingering health issues that needed attention first. My energy level was low. By early evening I was usually done for the day. I still had moments of dizziness, which were worrying. And the blood pressure issue hadn't gone away, although, oddly, it had reversed. In the hospital the problem had been low blood pressure, falling lower when I stood up; hence the Velcro corset. But now, when I checked the pressure, it was getting to be alarmingly high. I abandoned the corset; the pressure remained high and was approaching danger levels. The systolic number indicated the possibility of a stroke.

Then a lightbulb moment. I don't remember if the lightbulb appeared above my head or Eliza's, but I suspect it was over hers. We realized that one of the medications I'd been prescribed at Rusk was intended to boost the blood pressure. I had gone on taking it, because I had been given no guidance at the time of my discharge on when I should stop. I called my primary-care physician. "Stop taking it at once," he said. I stopped; and within a week or so, both the systolic and diastolic readings had dropped into the normal range.

Another case of iatrogenic disorderliness. Once again, medication had made me sick.

———

Eliza had been working hard at her computer, downloading all the footage we had shot, organizing it, and making a selection of representative clips. Finally, she asked me if I was ready to take a look.

"Yes," I said.

She set up a projector and a screen in the living room. She warned me that the images might upset me. It had been hard for her to look at them again. "The eye, the neck," she warned me. "It's pretty hard-core."

It was. I had no idea that I had looked that terrible, or that my voice had sounded that weak. It must have been terrifying for Eliza, Sameen, and Zafar to see me that way, and unbearably difficult for them to offer me their daily optimistic lies: "You're doing so well," "So much better than yesterday," and so forth. I wasn't doing well. I wasn't noticeably better day by day. I was someone on the very point of death who had somehow remained alive. That was all that the people who loved me had to hold on to—I was alive, and once the ventilator was removed it was probable that I would remain alive—and it enabled them to smile their loving, dishonest smiles. Eliza had been right to keep me away from mirrors. If I had known how bad I looked, how grave my injuries were, it might have been hard to summon the strength to go on.

The images rolled on. My bulging boiled-egg eye hung out of my face, the iris improbably perched on the swollen white at an impossible angle. The long horizontal gash in my blackened, swollen neck, the stab wounds next to it, the gashes in my face. It was a lot to take in. The brain didn't want to understand it. But there it all was on the screen, insisting on being seen.

I found that I was having an unexpected reaction to what I was seeing. Yes, it was shocking, but to my surprise I became quite calm as I watched, and was able to look at the material dispassionately. I said to Eliza, "I think it's because I look like this now, not like that, so I can be quite objective. Frankly, it makes me more impressed by my own recovery, because I was in really bad shape, and looked like shit. I looked like someone else."

That was the day on which we agreed that we should make a documentary film. Now that I'd seen what we had already made, I was in no doubt about its quality and force. At first, perhaps na-ively, we thought we might be able to make the film by ourselves, with the help of a researcher and an editor. But we saw sense soon enough. We were too close to the story, and while our footage could provide the unique, only-camera-in-the-room material that would be the film's reason for existence, we needed a professional filmmaker to add his or her vision for what else was needed and how it would be shaped. So we would find one. And Eliza's foot-age would be the spine, or perhaps the heart, of the film.

———

Eliza filmed me at home, talking about my reaction to seeing her record of my worst days, and slow recovery. "I looked like some-one else," I had told her. Start with that.

The most upsetting thing about the attack is that it has turned me once again into somebody I have tried very hard not to be. For more than thirty years I have refused to be defined by the fatwa and insisted on being seen as the author of my books—five before the fatwa and sixteen after it. I had just about managed it. When the last few books were published, people finally stopped asking me about the attack on *The Satanic Verses* and its author. And now here I am, dragged back into that unwanted subject. I think now I'll never be able to escape it. No matter what I've already written or may now write, I'll always be the guy who got knifed. The knife defines me. I'll fight a battle against that, but I suspect I will lose.

Living was my victory. But the meaning the knife had given my life was my defeat. In *Victory City,* my central character, Pampa Kampana, writes a mighty narrative poem in Sanskrit, named *Jayaparajaya,* meaning "Victory and Defeat." That could also be the title for the story of my life.

————

All of a sudden it was a new year, 2023. February was around the corner, and February had many meanings. In February, *Victory City* would be published in the English language worldwide, and many translations would follow swiftly after that. I have rarely enjoyed the actual moment of publication. It feels like undressing in public, which allows people to point and laugh. In an ideal world, when a book is published I would prefer to hide behind the furniture for a few weeks. But that isn't possible in the real world. And anyway, I had been hiding behind the furniture for six months. This February, it was time to show my face.

I had done a long interview with David Remnick for *The New Yorker,* my only contribution to the launch of the novel, since a book tour was out of the question. With the interview there was a photograph by Richard Burbridge. When the interview and picture were published, it was like a re-entry into the world after half a year in Limbo. February meant all that. Also, February 14 was the thirty-fourth anniversary of the fatwa. I had stopped remembering fatwa anniversaries, but now I had to start again.

But February 14 was also Valentine's Day, and Eliza and I decided to celebrate it by going out for our first restaurant meal in six months. We went with security, but we went. It felt like a profound moment. Hello, world, we were saying. We're back, and after our encounter with hatred, we're celebrating the survival of love. After the angel of death, the angel of life.

6

The A.

O n October 14, 1994, six years after the announcement of
his Nobel Prize, the eighty-two-year-old Egyptian writer
Naguib Mahfouz left home to walk to his favorite Cairo café for
his weekly meeting with his fellow writers and thinkers. As he
walked a car began crawling along beside him. He said afterward
that he thought it was probably a fan. It was not a fan. It was a
man who jumped out of the car and repeatedly stabbed Mahfouz in the neck. Mahfouz fell, and his assailant escaped. Fortunately, the great writer survived the attack, but it was an instance
of the "cultural terrorism" of which he had previously accused
Egyptian Islamist fundamentalists.

The possibility of such an attack had hung over Mahfouz's
head for many years. His novel *The Children of Gebelawi* (also
published under the title *Children of the Alley*), an allegory set in
a poor Cairo alley that describes the birth of the three great
monotheisms, Judaism, Christianity, and Islam, had been banned
for "offending Islam." At least one firebrand fanatical mullah had

declared that Mahfouz deserved to die. An Islamist death list was discovered and he was on it, near the top. But he "doesn't believe in bodyguards," his daughter told *The New York Times*. In his Nobel year, 1988, he was quoted as saying, "I walk to the coffee shop, and I don't look to the left or the right. And so what if they get me? I have lived my life and done what I wanted to do."

He survived, and lived for another twelve years, with the constant bodyguard protection he had refused earlier. His injuries were such that he could only write for a few minutes a day.

I have read that the fatwa against *The Satanic Verses,* which he had opposed, was the trigger for the attack against him. This is what he had written in my defense in the book *For Rushdie,* in which a hundred Muslim writers and intellectuals had spoken out on my behalf: "The veritable terrorism of which he is a target is unjustifiable, indefensible. One idea can only be opposed by other ideas. Even if the punishment is carried out, the idea as well as the book will remain." It grieves me to this day that these words may have put a knife into his neck long before another such knife entered mine. But Mahfouz was right. His ideas, and books, live on.

I can only hope mine will as well.

———

I often thought about what happened to Mahfouz without ever truly believing that something of the same kind might happen to me. I tried to imagine the cast of mind that would be willing to drive a blade into an old man's neck, an eminent old man, whose work was loved by many. I do not place myself on Naguib Mahfouz's level, but now I am obliged to consider the cast of mind of the man who was willing to murder me. Therefore, in this chapter I have recorded a conversation that never occurred, between myself and a man I met for only twenty-seven seconds of my life. In his photographs he is dressed in black-and-white prison clothing, and handcuffed. He is a serious-looking young man, but, then, most people would be serious in photographs taken after their arrest. Maybe in his private life he is good company, and tells jokes. But in my imagining of him he is a solitary figure, mostly keeping his own company. His ears stick out. He has a narrow face, and his hair and beard are both close-cropped. He bears a slight resemblance to the tennis player Novak Djokovic. He grew up in New Jersey, so maybe he would speak in the distinctive accents of a Jersey boy, but I will not attempt to reproduce that speech pattern here. In the imagined scenes below, I have traveled to Chautauqua County Jail and am seated at a metal table on a metal chair, both fastened to the ground, as is the chair in which he sits, handcuffed, shackled. He does not really want to talk to me, but as this is my imagination at work, he has no choice. His disposition is surly. He is not loquacious. Is his unexamined life worth living? I will ask him.

We are watched by prison officers and perhaps also by federal agents through a one-way mirror. It looks like an interrogation scene from the TV series *Law & Order*. (As a footnote, there's a serious *Law & Order* addiction going on in my home, so I'm well acquainted with the basics of American law enforcement as entertainment. The real thing is another thing, obviously. This imagined location is not the place for that discussion.)

How am I to approach him, the wielder of the knife? I circle him in my mind, I think of ways into the conversation. Should I talk to him about Iago, who destroyed his own life as well as Othello's and Desdemona's, merely because he was passed over for a promotion? I do want to ask the A. how he feels about ruining his own life, but I suspect Shakespeare may not be the best way in. I'm thinking, too, about more arcane moments in literature. The scene in André Gide's *Les Caves du Vatican* (The Vatican Cellars) in which a character named Lafcadio throws a man he has only just met out of a moving train and kills him, for no reason at all. Or Friedrich Dürrenmatt's *The Execution of Justice,* in which a man commits a murder in front of many witnesses and then insists on arguing his innocence to see "how reality might look if, instead of me, someone else had been the murderer." I abandon these thoughts quite quickly, even though they do seem to have some relevance. We aren't going to have a literary conversation.

I don't want to be too friendly. I don't feel friendly. But I don't want to be too unfriendly either. I want to open him up, if I can. Because a real meeting is improbable—make that impossible—I have to imagine my way into his head. I have to try to make him up, make him real. I don't know if I can.

There is a part of me that wants to run at him and punch him hard in the neck.

He has expressed no remorse. I'm not looking for an apology. I do wonder how he feels, now that he has had time to think things over. Has he had second thoughts? Or is he proud of himself? Would he do it again? He has been offered a reward by an organization in Iran. Does he hope to serve a sentence and then travel to receive his prize? His social media reveal his admiration for various Islamist radicals. Is he, in his own eyes, a hero, or just a young fellow from New Jersey who did what he felt he had to do?

Does he think of himself as an American?

I clear my throat, and begin.

———

First session.

Can we start with the word "disingenuous."

Why?

You used it to describe me to the *New York Post*. You said
you found me to be a disingenuous person.

Okay. So? You are.

Have you seen the movie *The Princess Bride*?

No. Yes. I don't know. Who cares? Why are you asking me
about movies?

There's a character, Vizzini, who is fond of the word "incon-
ceivable." He says it several times in the film. Five times,
I think. Finally, another character, Inigo Montoya, says to
him: "You keep using that word. I do not think it means
what you think it means." And so: Can I ask you about the
word "disingenuous"?

I see. You are condescending to me.

I'm asking you to tell me what you understand by the word.

It means you pretend to be telling the truth when you're not.

Yes, it does.

So—fuck you, Mr. Smartypants.

I have a second question. Let's say that you're right. Let's say
I do pretend to tell the truth when in fact I am deceiving
people.

This is what you do. Everybody knows it.

And is that, in your opinion, a reason to kill a person? How
   many people have you met in your life who were, in your
   opinion, disingenuous?

In America many people pretend to be honest, but they wear
   masks and lie.

And would that be a reason to kill them all?

Silence.

Have you ever thought of murdering other people?

No.

Even though you find many people in America to be disingenuous. Are you sure you never thought of killing anyone
   before?

Why would I tell you?

Your mother, for example. You said your mother didn't teach
   you properly about religion. Now she has disowned you.
   Is your mother disingenuous? She pretended to be honest
   but actually she was concealing the truth?

Silence.

Okay. Let's leave "disingenuous" and look at another word—
   the word "everybody."

That's stupid. It's an ordinary word.

Yes, it is. It's an ordinary word you used to make an allegation against me. I am dishonest, you said, and "everybody knows it."

I agree. Everybody knows it.

Can you tell me who everybody is?

You are asking questions to which you know the answers.

Indulge me.

Everybody is all good people. People who know the Devil when he comes to trick them. People who know right from wrong.

So, in your opinion, I am not only disingenuous, I am the Devil. Is that why it's right to kill me?

You are only a little devil—don't flatter yourself. But even a little devil is a devil.

And devils must be destroyed?

Yes.

These are views you have held for a long time? Or are these new ideas?

We used to live in a wrong way in our household. My mother, my sisters. I also. I was ignorant. I was asleep. Now I am awake.

What woke you up?

God woke me up.

How did He do it? Did you experience a revelation?

I'm not a prophet. The time of prophets is over. The revelation of God to Man is complete. I didn't see an angel. I
   studied. I learned.

From books? From people?

From Imam Yutubi.

Who is that?

You can find him on his YouTube channels. He has many
   faces, many voices. But they all tell the truth.

Tell me the truth.

The truth is that the truth has many enemies. Those
   who know the truth know also that it is precious, so
   many people want to make it cheap. Many want to per-
   secute the possessors of the truth. So it is necessary to
   defend it.

By any means necessary?

Yes. As we were taught by el-Hajj Malik el-Shabazz.

Malcolm X. Do you follow Malcolm X?

I follow God.

Do you know that Malcolm took that phrase from Frantz
Fanon?

I don't know any Fanon.

A Black intellectual from Martinique. And afterward Algeria.

He doesn't matter.

I studied the origins of your faith too, you know. At a British
university.

You learned nothing.

Why do you say that?

Your teachers, were they of the faith? Were they imams
learned in the law?

One was a French Marxist and the other, English, not religious.

You see? They had nothing to teach you, and so that's what
you learned.

Can I change the subject? Can we talk about your gym
membership?

You have a bad mind. A mind like a butterfly. It can't stay fo-
cused on what matters. It is an American mind.

But I am from India originally. From a secular Indian Muslim family. I have an Indian mind and later a British mind
   and now, maybe, yes, also an American mind.

"Secular" is a synonym for "liar." It is a sickness.

You're sure of that? Because my mother, for example, was a
   very truthful person.

She must have been ashamed to have you as a son. Your
   name is Muslim. Why do you keep this name? To keep
   this name is to lie. Your mother must have been ashamed
   to carry you in her womb. Your family must be ashamed
   to acknowledge you as their blood.

When she died in Pakistan, a newspaper said the people who
   went to her funeral should be ashamed.

You see? It is as I said.

Can we go back to the gym membership?

Why are you so obsessed about this?

The State of Fitness Boxing Club, yes? In North Bergen,
   New Jersey? You signed up for the premium package and
   took twenty-seven boxing classes. There's the number
   twenty-seven again. Twenty-seven classes, a twenty-seven-
   second attack. It would be even better if you were twenty-
   seven years old. Anyway. You're the quiet type. You didn't
   say much to anyone at the gym. Your mother said you
   were a quiet boy. But you did speak up the night before

you took a bus to Chautauqua. You emailed the gym and
canceled your membership.

So what.

I'd like to ask you this. You plainly knew you wouldn't be
coming back to your previous life. No more boxing lessons
in the gym, no more Imam Yutubi videos in your basement. You had a nocturnal lifestyle, your mother said, you
locked yourself away in your basement and cooked your
own meals. But when you canceled your gym membership
you knew that life was over. You were going to wreck your
own life as well as mine. Maybe you knew you were going
to be locked up, but not by yourself. Not in your basement. Somewhere else.

Okay, yes.

Or did you think you'd escape and go on the run? There
would be a manhunt but you'd cheat them all and get
across the Canadian border, which isn't very far from
Chautauqua? You had fake ID and no credit cards but a
fair amount of cash. Did you imagine getting a boat and
crossing Lake Erie, where the frontier is liquid, it's just an
imaginary line across the middle of the lake? Were you
going to start a new life in, oh, Vancouver?

I didn't know what would happen.

But you knew you weren't coming home. Goodbye to all
that. You had once thought to finish college and so on. No
more of that.

I guess so.

I'm trying to understand you. You were only twenty-four
    years old. Your whole life ahead of you. Why were you so
    ready to ruin it? *Your* life. Not mine. Yours.

Don't try to understand me. You aren't capable of under-
    standing me.

But I have to try, because for twenty-seven seconds we
    were profoundly intimate. You put on the mantle of
    Death itself, and I was Life. This is a profound con-
    joining.

I was ready to do it because I was serving God.

You're sure of that. This is something your God wanted you
    to do.

Imam Yutubi was very clear. Those who are against God
    have no right to live. We have the right to end them.

But most people on Earth do not follow your God. If they
    are for other gods, or no god, do you have the right to end
    them too? Two billion people following your God. Six bil-
    lion others. What do you think about them?

It depends.

On what?

On how they behave.

And disingenuous behavior deserves death.

You can say that, yes.

Let me ask you something about your beliefs. Do you believe that everything that comes from God is sacred? Or,
another word, holy?

Yes. Of course. The Word of God is holy and so are His
deeds.

The gift of life is a deed of God, would you agree?

Yes.

Then how is it right for a man to take away what God has
given? Is that not for God to decide?

You are trying to confuse me. I see it. You are using tricks as
a devil does. You don't even believe in God. An atheist is
the lowest of the low. You don't deserve to talk to me. You
are not my equal.

I want to understand you. This is my difficulty. The reasons
you give don't seem strong enough to drive a young man,
a young man who never was violent before, a young man
who wasn't even very good at boxing, an amateur . . . to
drive such a man to sacrifice the rest of his life just to
murder a stranger. The decision to murder—to be a
murderer—is not a small decision. And yet you went
about it seriously, carefully, in a committed fashion. You
made detailed plans. But you never did anything like it
before. What changed you?

If you believed in Heaven you would understand.

Tell me.

You would understand that this life, here in this world, is
    unimportant. It is only a waiting room in which the best
    we can do is to follow God, and then after this life we will
    have the life eternal. So what does it matter where I
    spend these years? When you are burning in hellfire I
    will be in the perfumed garden. I will have my attendant
    spirits, my beautiful houris, untouched by man or djinn.
    It is written: "Which of the Lord's blessings would you
    deny?"

Written where?

In the Book.

I'd like to talk about books.

There's only one book worth talking about.

Let me tell you about a book about a book. It's written
    by the Turkish author Pamuk, and called *The New Life*.
    In this book there's a book that has no name, and we
    do not know anything about what's written on its pages.
    But everyone who opens this book has their whole life
    changed. After they read the book they are not the
    same as they were before. Do you know a book like
    that?

Of course. It is the book containing the Word of God, as
    given by the Archangel to the Prophet.

Did the Prophet write it down immediately?

He came down from the mountain and recited, and whoever was nearby wrote it down on whatever came to hand.

And he recited with complete accuracy. What the Archangel said: word for word. And then they wrote it down with complete accuracy also. Word for word.

That is obvious.

And what happened to these pages?

After the Prophet's life ended, his Companions put them in order, and that is the Book.

And they put them in order with complete accuracy.

Every true believer knows this. Only the godless would question this, and they don't matter.

Can I ask you a question about the nature of God?

He is all-encompassing. All-knowing. He is All.

It is in your tradition, is it not, that there is a difference between your God and the God of the other People of the Book, the Jews and the Christians. They believe, as it says in their books, that God created Man in His own image.

They are wrong.

Because, if they were right, then God might have some re-
    semblance to men? He might look like a man? He might
    have a mouth, and a voice, and be able to use it to speak
    to us?

But this is not correct.

Because, in your tradition, the idea of God is that He is so
    far superior to Man, so much more exalted, that He
    shares no human qualities.

Exactly. For once you are not talking garbage.

What would you say were human qualities?

Our bodies. How we look and how we are.

Is love a human quality? Is the desire for justice? Is mercy?
    Does God have those?

I am not a scholar. Imam Yutubi is a scholar. He is many-
    headed and many-voiced. I follow him. I have learned ev-
    erything from him.

I don't mean to ask you for scholarship. You agree that your
    God has no human qualities, according to your own tradi-
    tion. Let me just ask this. Isn't language a human quality?
    To have a language, God would have to have a mouth, a
    tongue, vocal cords, a voice. He would have to look like a
    man. *In His own image.* But you agree that God is not like
    that.

So what?

So if God is above language—so far above it as He is so far above all that is merely human—then how did the words of your Book come into being?

The Angel understood God and brought the Message in a way that the Messenger could understand, and the Messenger received it.

Was the Message in Arabic?

That's how the Messenger received it and how his Companions wrote it down.

Can I ask you something about translation?

You do this too much. We are going in one direction and then you swerve across the road and start driving the other way. Not only a butterfly but a bad driver.

I only want to suggest that when the Archangel understood the Word of God and brought it to the Messenger in a way that the Messenger could understand, he was translating it. God communicated in the way that God communicates, which is so far above human understanding that we cannot even begin to comprehend it, and the Angel made it comprehensible to the Messenger, by delivering it in human speech, which is not the speech of God.

The Book is the uncreated Word of God.

But we agreed that God has no words. In which case, what
we read is an interpretation of God. And so maybe there
could be other interpretations? Maybe your way, your Yutubi's way, is not the only way? Maybe there is no one correct way?

You are a snake.

Can I ask in what language you read the Book? In the first
language or another?

I read it in this inferior tongue in which we are speaking
now.

Another translation.

I understood it through the many hours of instruction I received from Imam Yutubi.

In your nocturnal life, locked in your basement, looking at
your laptop. In between playing video games and watching Netflix.

Of course.

And what you received from your many-headed imam were
further interpretations. More acts, we might say, of translation.

What you are saying makes no sense. It is irrelevant to anything that matters.

I'm trying to suggest to you that, even according to your own
tradition, there is uncertainty. Some of your own early
philosophers have suggested this. Your Yutubis from the
centuries before YouTube. They say everything can be interpreted, even the Book. It can be interpreted according
to the times in which the interpreter lives. Literalism is a
mistake.

That is not so. The Word is the Word. To question that is to
question the meaning of life. Of the stability of the universe.

Let me ask one last question, and then we can rest until tomorrow. Have you ever been to Jerusalem?

No.

Because in Jerusalem, as you know, there stands the Dome
of the Rock.

The Haram al-Sharif. Al-Aqsa.

You know, I haven't been to Jerusalem either. But I have
been told that on the walls of that mosque are certain in-
scriptions of verses taken from your Book.

Yes, naturally.

And I have been told that, curiously, some of these verses are
a little different from those in the Book you now have.

That is impossible.

It's impossible, right? Because the mosque is very old. So what would that mean? If those old words on the walls are not exactly the words you have in your pages?

It means you're not telling the truth. You're lying. As usual.

I won't argue. I haven't seen this for myself.

You say what you write are "fictions." Which is another word for "lies."

Like "secular."

Exactly. You make your living as a liar.

Let's stop there. Maybe we'll get on better tomorrow.

———

Second session.

Can we talk this morning about foreign travel? Do you like to travel abroad? Do you believe that travel broadens the mind?

More stupid questions. I have no interest in tourism. The world is the same everywhere. The question is, can one see it as it is. Not many people can do that.

But in 2018 you did leave America. You went to Lebanon.

I went to visit my father. That is the opposite of tourism.

They say Beirut was very beautiful then, before the explosion
of 2020. You are lucky to have seen it. A city of great cul-
ture, great civilization, a liberal, open city, known as the
Paris of the East.

I didn't spend time in Beirut. And you are romanticizing.
Maybe you are ignorant of the conflicts in that part of the
world, the civil war, the wars involving Syria and Israel.
My father does not live in Beirut. He lives in a village near
the border.

Your mother says that at first you didn't like it there and
wanted to come back right away. But you stayed a month
and came back changed. So it seems travel did affect your
mind.

My mother can say whatever she wants.

Your former stepfather was very surprised by what you had
done. He wept, and said you were smart and had a very
good heart and wouldn't touch anybody. So it seems you
did change. Something happened to you there that altered your whole personality.

Silence.

Your neighbors in Fairview, New Jersey, describe you as a
loner who didn't socialize much. But in Lebanon, I'm
guessing, you did socialize. I'm guessing you met people.

Yes, of course.

What can you say about the people you met?

They were strong. Powerful. They understood the world.
      They saw it as it is.

They were religious? More religious than your mother and
      sisters?

They were men. They had real men's understanding of the
      faith. They took no shit from anybody. They served God
      and fought for Him.

They opened your eyes.

They opened my heart.

Then you came home and moved into your mother's base-
      ment and stopped talking to her and your sisters. What
      did you do down there?

Like you said. I played video games and watched Netflix.
      And listened to Imam Yutubi.

And this is how you lived for four years.

I was thinking.

About what?

About how many enemies we have. It is as you yourself said.
      One-quarter of the human race—two billion people—is
      us, the other three-quarters is not us, and there is hatred

for us. You see it everywhere in America. I saw it in Lebanon also. The enemy is all around, and we must learn to
fight. Two billion against six billion. We must learn to
overcome such odds.

I want to explore this, the idea of the enemy.

Of course. Because it is you.

And the idea of the enemy justifies violence against such
persons.

The enemy is violence in human form. Violence walking and
talking and acting. In a certain way, the enemy is not
human. It is a devil. How should one proceed against such
entities? You know the answer. Because the entity is you.

You believe I am violence in human form. You spent four
years learning this.

You are unimportant. I learned many things. Finally, I asked
myself, what was I personally prepared to do against the
enemy? Only then did I begin to think about people like
you.

What are people like me like?

You are hated by two billion people. That is all that it is necessary to know. How must that feel, to be so hated? You
must feel like a worm. Beneath all your smart talk, you
know you are less than a worm. To be crushed beneath
our heel. You talk about travel to other countries, but you
can't set foot in half the countries of the world because

there is so much hatred for you there. Say something
about that, why don't you.

I have learned a lot about demonization, that's true. I know
that it is possible to construct an image of a man, a second
self, that bears very little resemblance to the first self, but
this second self gains credibility because it is repeated
over and over again, until it begins to feel real, more real
than the first self. I believe it's this second self that you
have gotten to know, against whom your sense of an
enemy is aimed. To answer your question, I know I am
not that second self. I am myself, and I turn away from
hatred, and toward love.

No, that is fakery. What I know of you is real. Everybody
knows that.

There's a story by Hans Christian Andersen about a shadow
that separates itself from a man and becomes more real
than the man. In the end the shadow marries a princess
and the real man is executed for being a fake.

I don't care about stories, as I told you before.

What if I said to you, at the heart of the book I wrote, which
you hate even though you only read two pages of it, is an
East London Muslim family running a café-restaurant,
portrayed with real love? What if I told you that before
that I wrote a book in which I placed a sympathetically
drawn Muslim family at the heart of the narrative of Indian and Pakistani independence? What if I said to you,
when plans for a mosque near the 9/11 Ground Zero site
were opposed by some New Yorkers, I defended the

mosque's right to be there? What if I said to you, I have
consistently opposed the present Indian administration's
sectarian ideology, of which Muslims are the main vic-
tims? And what if I said to you, I once wrote a book in
which the condition of Kashmiri Muslims, and of a young
Kashmiri man who turns to jihad, was sympathetically
portrayed? In a way, I wrote that book, *Shalimar the
Clown*, about you before I knew you, and, writing it, I
knew that character is destiny—so that, in your case,
there's something I'm trying to get at, something in you
beneath all the Yutubi noise that made it possible for you
to pick up the knife.

It doesn't matter what you say to me. We know who you are.
   If you think you can win us over, then you are a fool.

Very well. In that case, that is the kind of fool I am.

Silence.

What if I said to you, the reason why I, and people like me,
   have always opposed the death penalty is that there are
   many wrongful convictions, and if the wrongfully convicted person is executed then the matter cannot be recti-
   fied?

Don't lie. You oppose the death penalty because you have
   been rightfully convicted and you are afraid to die.

What if I said to you, there are Muslim writers who find my
   book, that book which you hate after reading two pages,
   to be beautiful and true? What if I said to you, they want
   to reclaim my book as a capacious work of art? Is there

any possibility that you might consider the possibility that
there are other ways of seeing what I do, what I have
done? You wanted to be an executioner. What if later you
read these writers and understand that you might have
been wrong?

It isn't important. I'm not really a reader. But I know what I
know.

You're going to have a lot of time to read. I don't think you'll
have Netflix or video games where you're going.

I don't care.

Your favorite video game is *Call of Duty*, I imagine?

It's your imagination.

What if I told you that my younger son—my son who is not
even two years older than you—is an expert player of that
game? Maybe you even played against each other somewhere out there in the gamer universe? How does that
make you feel? That maybe, behind all the pseudonyms,
you might have been friends? Friendly adversaries? Or
even on the same team?

It makes me feel nothing.

The writer Jodi Picoult says this in her novel *My Sister's
Keeper:* "If you meet a loner, no matter what they tell you,
it's not because they enjoy solitude. It's because they have
tried to blend into the world before, and people continue
to disappoint them." I find this helpful. I see you now at

twenty-four, already disappointed by life, disappointed in
your mother, your sisters, your fathers, your lack of boxing
talent, your lack of any talent at all; disappointed in the
bleak future you saw stretching ahead of you, for which
you refused to blame yourself. But you needed to blame,
you wanted very much to blame, and all that loose blame
flooded through and around you, and then something, a
tweet, a video, who knows, directed all that lifetime of
blame in my direction, and it settled on my head, and you
began to make your plan.

Silence.

I'm just wondering. You lived a lot of your nighttime life in
imaginary universes. In those universes, the universe of
Call of Duty, death is everywhere, but it isn't real. You
kill many, many people, but you also kill nobody. You go:
Run kill shelter. Run kill hide. When you went to Chautauqua, was that a move in the game? It would be a killing in which nobody died? Or maybe you didn't even
know you would do it, because you would have to cross
the border between the gamer world and this one and
maybe that was too much? You could bring the gamer
knife, but in this world it would really cut and wound
and really kill. I think you weren't even sure you were
really going to do it until I came out on stage and you
got up out of your seat and started to run. And then your
running feet took you across the point of no return and
there was no way to stop. You were right in front of me
and there I was: reality. Real honest-to-goodness reality
standing on its own two feet, facing you, looking you in
the eye. There was me and there were all your other realities too, your loneliness, your failures, your disap-

pointments, your need to blame, your four years of indoctrination, your idea of the Enemy. I was all those things, and you started stabbing and you thought it was terrifying, it felt good to you but terrifying at the same time. I'm sure you were scared. You were scared to death. Because the one who had lived in fictions was you, and now you were facing the consequences of being led by your fictions into the real world, which is to say toward murder, and toward your own ruined life.

Silence.

———

Third session.

Allow me to ask: Do you have a girlfriend?

What kind of a question is that?

Ordinary question to ask an ordinary guy. Have you ever been in love?

I love God.

Yes, but human beings? I know you told me about your houris in Heaven. But Heaven is still some way away. No houris anytime soon. Anybody down here?

None of your business.

I'll take that as a no. How about a boyfriend? I heard you talk about your admiration for the real men in Lebanon. How about real men in Jersey?

Don't be disgusting.

So—another negative. Just to check: *never*? Nobody in your whole life? You're arousing in me an unexpected emotion.

What emotion.

Pity.

You pity *me*? No, no. I. I pity *you*. Also, you are intrusive and rude.

I'll tell you what's intrusive and rude. A twenty-seven-second knife attack. That's what. In my view it gives me some license to ask you personal questions. What's the difference between a virgin and an incel?

Fuck off.

An incel is angry about being a virgin. You're an angry guy. Six billion enemies, zero friends, zero-plus lovers. Furious. So many resentments. I'm just wondering who you were really trying to kill. Some girl who brushed you off? Some guy at the gym or on the Israeli border? Maybe your mother? That's what one of my friends thinks, and she's a lot smarter than me. Was I the proxy murderee? Whose face did you see when you were stabbing me?

This conversation is over.

No, no. The point about this is, it's happening in my head, so
it's not over until my head says it is. You don't even have
to think of things to say. I'll put the words into your
mouth.

Then they will be worthless.

I'm thinking about some other killers who were motivated
by religion: the men in the hijacked airplanes on September 11, 2001, and the men in Mumbai murderously at-
tacking the Taj Palace and Oberoi hotels, a Jewish
Chabad center, and the much-loved Leopold Café, on
November 26, 2008. I do not recall any wife or lover ever
being associated with any of them, any horrified life-
partner at once denouncing and mourning them. Maybe
men in love find it harder to carry out such cold-blooded
attacks. Maybe such persons' solitude is a necessary pre-
condition for their willingness to do such deeds. And
maybe you, dear A., are a member of that group of solitary killers.

If this is what you choose to believe, believe it. However, my
emotional life has nothing to do with my choices.

And now let's talk about America.

Why?

Just checking to see if I can find the Jersey boy under the Islamist radical. You like Springsteen? Follow football? Jets
guy or Giants guy? Basketball? Did you give up on the
Nets when they moved to Brooklyn? How about Bon

Jovi? Queen Latifah? Meryl Streep?—Well, I withdraw
Meryl Streep. I don't think she's your type.

I'm not answering.

Then let's move up to the national level. Americana. Don't
    you think murder is the American sport par excellence?
    Americans murder one another in large quantities every
    single day. We murder everyone—children, adults, Jews,
    you name it. We murder in malls and hospitals and places
    of worship. I say "we" because I'm a citizen too. You were
    born here, I wasn't, so you could argue that I'm not as
    American as you. Certainly I have never thought about
    killing anyone, much less made a plan. But you made a
    plan. However, you failed to carry it out successfully.
    That's not very American of you, now that I think of it.
    Maybe that's your Lebanese side showing itself. What do
    you think?

I think you're full of shit.

Let me ask you a serious question. What do you think is the
    value of a single human life?

The value in what terms?

I'm not talking cash value. I'm not asking how much you'd
    charge per hit. It's more of a moral question. Life: In your
    opinion, valuable, or cheap?

That depends on whose life it is.

And who sets that value?

Whoever has power over whoever else. You don't have
power, your life ain't worth shit.

So you, with the knife, you had the power, and made your
valuation of my life.

You could say that.

But now you're in jail and I'm asking the questions. Surprising, no?

Yeah. I'm surprised.

What value do you put on your own life? I'm wondering. I've
been wanting to ask you about Socrates, who said that the
unexamined life isn't worth living. So it follows that only
the examined life *is* worth living. My question: Do you ex-
amine your life? Do you look inward every day and try to
decide what you think about what you do?

That sounds like vanity to me. Sounds like fucking narcis-
sism. "Oh, let me look inward because it's all about me,
life. I'm the important one."

And you're not?

I've been trying to get this through to you. I'm not important. You're extra-not-important. What's important is to
serve God. If you're His servant, then that's important.
Listen: At school there's this experiment with iron filings

and a magnet. When you point the magnet, all the iron filings fall in line. They all point in the same direction. That's what I'm telling you. The magnet is God. If you're made of iron, you'll point in the right direction. And the iron is faith.

I begin to understand. You want to be a servant. You went looking for a master or an idea that was bigger than you, and you could bow down before it. You didn't want to be free. You wanted to submit.

You still don't get it. Only submission leads to freedom. That's the fucking point.

Thank you. I have a little more to ask you about. But it will wait.

Let me go. Let me out of here. Is this your revenge, to keep me imprisoned in your head?

This isn't a prison. Maybe it's a school.

You have nothing to teach me.

That's where we are. A place where the teacher cannot teach and the student cannot learn. And it's even unclear who is the student and who the instructor.

For all eternity.

Eternity's a long time. Let's just say, it's a life sentence.

Fourth and final session.

In "The Faith of a Rationalist," Bertrand Russell has this to
   say: "Men tend to have the beliefs that suit their passions.
   Cruel men believe in a cruel God, and use their belief to
   excuse their cruelty. Only kindly men believe in a kindly
   God, and they would be kindly in any case." This sounds
   convincing, but in your case, dear A., it doesn't quite seem
   to fit. How old were you when you went to see your father
   in Lebanon? Nineteen? A lonely boy, fatherless for much
   of your life, a boy with a void inside, easily led, easily
   shaped, wanting leading and shaping, but not a cruel
   youth. A "smart boy with a good heart who wouldn't touch
   anybody." So the question arises: Can such a child, barely
   an adult, be taught cruelty? Was the cruelty always there
   in some inner cave, waiting for the right words to release
   it? Or could it actually be planted in the virgin soil of your
   half-made character, take root, and flourish? Those who
   knew you were surprised by what you did. The murderer
   in you had not previously shown his face. That virgin self
   needed four years of Imam Yutubi to become what he,
   what you, became.

You don't know me. You'll never know me.

There's a thing I used to say back in the day, when catastro-
   phe rained down upon *The Satanic Verses* and its author:
   that one way of understanding the argument over that
   book was that it was a quarrel between those with a sense
   of humor and those without one. I see you now, my failed

murderer, *hypocrite assassin, mon semblable, mon frère.*
You could try to kill because you didn't know how to
laugh.

The imagined conversation is over. I no longer have the energy
to imagine him, just as he never had the ability to imagine me.
But there are still things I would wish to say to him, even though
I do not believe he has the ability to hear them.

The most important of these things is that art challenges or-
thodoxy. To reject or vilify art because it does that is to fail to
understand its nature. Art sets the artist's passionate personal
vision against the received ideas of its time. Art knows that received ideas are the enemies of art, as Flaubert told us in *Bou-
vard and Pécuchet.* Clichés are received ideas and so are
ideologies, both those which depend on the sanction of invisible sky gods and those which do not. Without art, our ability
to think, to see freshly, and to renew our world would wither
and die.

Art is not a luxury. It stands at the essence of our humanity,
and it asks for no special protection except the right to exist.

It accepts argument, criticism, even rejection. It does not accept violence.

And in the end, it outlasts those who oppress it. The poet
Ovid was exiled by Augustus Caesar, but the poetry of Ovid
has outlasted the Roman Empire. The poet Mandelstam's life
was ruined by Joseph Stalin, but his poetry has outlasted the
Soviet Union. The poet Lorca was murdered by the thugs of
General Franco, but his art has outlasted the fascism of the
Falange.

Sometimes, one stumbles upon the words one thinks one needs, words that sound like the right words, even though they come from a writer one does not often think about and he is talking about a philosopher one does not read. These words are by Joseph Campbell, and he's talking about Nietzsche:

> The idea came to him [Nietzsche] of what he called "the love of your fate." Whatever your fate is, whatever the hell happens, you say, "This is what I need." . . . Any disaster you can survive is an improvement in your character, your stature, and your life.

After a while one realizes that what is being said here is a cliché, which probably isn't true. To express it in ordinary English: what doesn't kill you makes you stronger.

But does it? Does it really?

7

Second Chance

Milan Kundera, who died as I was writing this book, believed that life is a one-shot affair. You can't revise what happens. There are no second drafts. This was what he meant by the "unbearable lightness of being," which, he once said, could be the title of every book he ever wrote, and which could be liberating as well as unbearable. I had always agreed with this idea, but the attack of August 12 changed my mind. As I recovered from my wounds, both physical and psychological, I was far from sure that I would emerge from the experience stronger. I was just happy to be emerging from the experience alive. Whether stronger or weaker, it was too soon to tell. What I did know was that, thanks to a combination of luck, the skill of surgeons, and loving care, I had been given a second chance. I was getting what Kundera believed impossible—a second shot at life. I had beaten the odds. So now the question was: When you are given a second opportunity, what do you do with it? How do you use it? What should you do the same way, what might you do differently? I found myself thinking about Raymond Carver, and his poem "Gravy," which was about being told he had six months to live and then getting an extra decade of life. The poem had been written when he knew his time had finally run out. Lung cancer had him in its grip and wasn't going to let him go.

> ... *"Don't weep for me,"*
> *he said to his friends. "I'm a lucky man.*
> *I've had ten years longer than I or anyone*
> *expected. Pure gravy. And don't forget it."*

That was a good way to think of it. Every day of life, now, was gravy. Thank you, Ray. And I too can "call myself beloved," I have felt myself "beloved on the earth." Hated, yes, that too, but "beloved" trumps all hate.

Eliza and I decided that we would not think in the long term. We would be grateful for each day of gravy and live it as fully as we could. We would ask ourselves each day: How are we today? Where do things stand right now? What would be good to do today, okay to do again, and if so how would we go about doing it, and with whom? What sort of thing should we hold off doing until our instincts said otherwise? Short-term-ism became our philosophy. The horizon was too far away. We couldn't see that far.

In the week before our Valentine's Day celebration, *Victory City* was published, and its reception gladdened my heart. I have had good publications and less good ones, but this was special, partly for obvious reasons—that I was still around to witness it—but mostly for what may sound less obvious: that the reviews and commentary about the book were not driven by sympathy or pity, not "Poor Salman, let's be nice to him" pieces, but serious engagements with the book as a work of art. I normally forget good reviews and remember bad ones, but this time I avoided such negativity. Most of all, I was proud of the book's success in India, where it was spoken about with knowledge, understanding, excitement, and love. Probably my best-received book in the country of my birth since *Midnight's Children* long ago. Distinguished Indian critics writing in Western journals were also laudatory. It was a dream publication, and gave me hope, and strength.

I couldn't do much to support the book's publication. It was extraordinary, however, to see my fellow writers stepping in to fill the void. I watched Neil Gaiman and Margaret Atwood discussing *Victory City* with Erica Wagner in a streamed program watched by a large audience, in which Sarita Choudhury read extracts from the book better than I could have dared to hope anyone would read them. At the Hay Festival in the U.K., Elif Shafak, Douglas Stuart, and again Atwood had another celebratory discussion about the novel. Everywhere I looked, as I contemplated my next steps back into the world, I felt the reassuring arms of friends around my shoulders.

I went to Brooklyn to visit Paul Auster in his Park Slope home. What a year he had had. The death of his granddaughter followed by the death of his son. And now cancer. He had begun chemotherapy, and his hair had fallen out. Paul had always had beautiful hair. Now his head was hidden beneath a hat. He had lost weight. But his spirits were good. He was to have four doses of chemo at three-week intervals, as well as immunotherapy. The hope was that this would reduce the tumor. After that there would be a month or six weeks of recovery from the weakening effects of the chemotherapy, and then, he hoped, surgery. The surgery would need to remove two of the three lobes of one lung. I reminded him that the playwright turned Czech president Václav Havel, also a heavy smoker, ended up with only half of one lung after his surgery, but kept going pretty well on that. He laughed and said he hoped to do better than that. It was good to see him and hear him laugh. I was glad to see his optimism. But cancer was sneaky. One could only hope for the best.

————

The big news—for me, anyway—was that, after half a year of nothingness, the writing juices had indeed started to flow again. I didn't make the connection then, but, looking back at that time now, I think that perhaps my careful re-entry into ordinary life helped. I wrote the proposal for the book you are now reading and my publishers liked it. I was, once again, an author with a book to write.

To be frank, it was and is a book I'd much rather not have needed to write. There was and still is another book in my head, which I had thought might follow *Victory City*, a novel about a mysterious and enigmatic College, and to prepare for that book I had been rereading Thomas Mann's *The Magic Mountain* and Franz Kafka's *The Castle*, both great books about mysterious and enigmatic microcosms of the sort I hoped my College might become. I tried hard to avoid the elephant-in-the-room cliché, but the unavoidable truth was that there was a fucking enormous mastodon in my workroom, waving its trunk and snorting and stinking quite a bit. I had written about comic-absurdist mastodons in my novel *Quichotte*, about people in New Jersey turning into mastodons, in fact, and now here, with its own Jersey connection, was a beast of my very own, insisting on being reckoned with.

This book is that reckoning. I tell myself it's my way of taking ownership of what happened, making it mine—making it my *work*. Which is a thing I know how to do. Dealing with a murder attack is not a thing I know how to do. A book about an attempted murder might be a way for the almost-murderee to get to grips with the event.

———

It's hard to write about post-traumatic stress disorder at any time, because, well, there's trauma involved, and a lot of stress, and a consequential disorder in the self. It's harder when two of you, you and your beloved wife, are experiencing it at the same time but in different ways. And it's really hard to do it with one eye and one and a half hands, because the physicality of the writing, its awkwardness, reminds you at every stroke of the keyboard of the cause of your pain. The hand feels like it's inside a glove, and it kind of crackles inside when moved. The eye . . . is an absence with an immensely powerful presence.

My way of trying to deal with PTSD was to claim, most of the time, that I was okay. I told my therapist, "I don't know what good it does to complain." He laughed. "Don't you know that the reason you're here is to complain?" After that I tried to let things out, but it wasn't easy. It's against my nature. Eliza is different. I could see every day how shaken she was, how far she had been knocked out of her happy place, and how hard she was trying to remain functional, loving, and present. All we could do for each other was to give one another a caring and supportive environment and to grind our way through until the storm clouds lifted.

There were moments when the pressure built up too much. "I need to go away," Eliza said. "I need time by myself to think and take care of myself and heal." I agreed, and called the manager of a Caribbean resort where we had stayed together in happier days. "Of course," he said. "We will care for her very well." It was hard to see her go, but it was obvious she needed it. And her multiple daily FaceTime calls showed me that her face was returning to itself, the tension was fading. The Caribbean magic was working.

It would obviously be too simple to say that a change of scene fixed everything, but it gave her a much-needed infusion of optimism.

As for me, there were days, especially when I was alone, when it was hard to get out of bed, and easy to be overwhelmed by negative thinking: *Is this it, am I finished, has the attack just taken too much out of me, and maybe it is killing me, slowly, even though it looks like I've made such a great recovery; maybe the knife is still inside me, traveling toward my heart* . . . But I was able to shake these thoughts off. And I started thinking about travel too.

In my life before the attack, I would fly to London many times a year to be with family and old friends, and for book publications as well. Now I didn't know how any of that would work. My family was worried about my security. I understood that everyone needed to be reassured. So I did something I hadn't done in a long time. I emailed my Special Branch contact officer at Scotland Yard.

In the old days, the Special Branch was the plainclothes division of the Metropolitan Police, which offered protection to politicians and other individuals deemed to be at serious risk. It was separate from the royal protection squad, which looked after the royal family. There had always been a little bit of (almost) good-natured needling rivalry between the two squads. But now they had been united under a single umbrella, the Royal and Special Protection Unit, or RaSP. For many years now, their attitude to me had been: If you're visiting for private reasons, then we don't need to be involved. If you're doing any public event, we'll come along with you to those. So, when I had a book coming out, and did a live event with an audience in London or else-where, at the Hay Festival, for example, protection officers came with me and, in a very low-key way, took care of things. But otherwise my life was my own.

I wrote to my contact: "In the light of what has happened, I wonder what would be your position if I came to visit England." I received a prompt reply, inquiring solicitously after my health, expressing the horror of everyone at the Yard at what had hap-pened, and saying that the decision would rest with the Home Office committee that decided who received protection and at what level. The RaSP would take the case before the committee as soon as possible.

The decision came gratifyingly soon. It hadn't taken the com-mittee long to decide, I was told, and the unanimous agreement had been that I should once again receive twenty-four-hour fully armed protection when in the U.K. A protection team would meet Eliza and me off the plane and be with us until we got back on a plane to leave. Everyone in my family was delighted. I felt deeply gratified that the U.K. wanted to be protective. But it also felt like slipping back into a past I had escaped over twenty years ago, when the "threat level" assessment had dropped to the point at which protection was no longer deemed necessary. Well, there was nothing for it but to be grateful. And I was.

"Just to reassure you," I was told, "we have no knowledge of any threat against you in the U.K. But the trouble is, there can always be one crazy individual, and it's hard to have all of those on our radar." A statement that was simultaneously reassuring and not reassuring.

I was worried about other things. In the bad old days, some airlines were too afraid to carry me. It might also have been dif-ficult to find accommodation. If any of that old unpleasantness came back it would be very hard for me to travel. But something had changed. Airlines had no problems, hotels were willing to welcome us, the country's arms were open wide. I was no longer a person to fear. Affection had replaced fear in the public mind. That meant a very great deal.

We landed in London on the morning of Thursday, March 23, 2023, and were greeted by the smiling face of Barry, our protection team leader. My instant reaction was of familiarity and relief. I knew how this went. My family and friends all remembered too, and were happy that I was being kept safe. For Eliza it was a little more difficult. She had no memory of the bad old days, and was understandably ill-at-ease at being surrounded by armed officers and shown into armored cars and told, Don't open the door, it's too heavy, we will open it for you. And the windows didn't open, because they were made of bulletproof material and were at least an inch thick.

I tried to make light of the situation. "We could imagine that we are rich enough to have personal chauffeurs," I ventured.

"No," she said. "It doesn't feel like that at all."

"Or we could think of all the money we'll be saving on Ubers," I said.

She gave me a look. I knew that look. It meant, stop being stupid. So I stopped. And as the days went by, she did get a little more used to it.

It was different this time. In the bad old days they wanted me to be "invisible," and so they didn't like the idea of my going to public places (such as restaurants), and if I went to visit family or friends at their homes, then one or often two officers would have to sit inside with me. And there was a persistent undercurrent of disapproval, not from my protection teams but from their bosses: a tabloidish belief that my problems were my fault and now I was costing too much money. This time the approach was much friendlier. I could go where I wished, and they would take care of things. And at people's homes, they waited for us outside. I felt more than protected. I felt appreciated.

Those ten days in London were emotional for everyone. Milan came to see me and said, "You look so much better than when I last saw you." Yes, I protested, but that was five months ago, and you've been seeing me on FaceTime all the time. "It's not the same," he said. Sameen felt the same way. We had last been together seven months ago, in that trauma ward in Erie, when I had been at my weakest and worst. Again, seeing me in person was "real" in a way that digital images were not. And there was the joy of seeing my little granddaughter, Rose, and of old friends. Simple things that meant everything. Also, it was good to see *Victory City* prominently displayed everywhere, and to hear good things about it from our friends.

Eliza received a copy of the U.K. galleys of her novel. On the last page of the acknowledgments, I found these words:

> Salman, let our love show this impossible world that nothing is impossible. I love you with every heart and story that has ever lived in me and every story that is to come. Salman—my joy, my home, my joy, my dream, and my miracle—*Always*.

It was the most beautiful declaration of love I had ever read, let alone received.

By the time we returned to New York I thought I was pretty clear that this was what my second chance at life should concentrate on: love, and work.

———

After a long silence, I had reactivated my Twitter account to help with the launch of *Victory City*, retweeting reviews, and so on. But Twitter is a poisoned well, and if you dip a bucket into it you draw up your share of filth. When it offered me an Oxford professor's view that those defending me had a "neoliberal idea of free speech," I could set that aside with no more than a shrug. But there were also various Muslim voices celebrating what had happened to me, hoping I lost my other eye, and comparing me, in my monocular condition, to the figure of the Dajjal, the one-eyed "false Messiah" of Muslim demonology, who first pretends to be a prophet and later also claims to be God. I stood "revealed," I was informed, as the Dajjal I truly was. Also, I looked deformed, hideous, like a monster, and so on. It was unnecessary to allow this trash into my head. It had nothing to do with love or work. Happily, without any regrets, I deleted the Twitter app from my phone.

I continued to think about the conflict of narratives that had dominated my public life for so long—one narrative in which I was respected, another in which I was detested—and I began to see this conflict as part of a wider battle of stories that bedevils us all. On May 13, 2022, PEN America had convened a unique international gathering of writers at the United Nations to discuss how writers might best respond to a world in crisis—meaning the war in Ukraine, but not only that. I was asked to speak briefly to the gathering. This is what I then said:

> We are engaged in a world war of stories—a war between incompatible versions of reality—and we need to learn how to fight it.
>
> A tyrant has arisen in Russia and brutality engulfs Ukraine, whose people, led by a satirist turned hero, offer heroic resistance, and are already creating a legend of freedom. The tyrant creates false narratives to justify his assault—the Ukrainians are Nazis, and Russia is menaced by Western conspiracies. He seeks to brainwash his own citizens with such lying stories.
>
> Meanwhile, America is sliding back towards the Middle

Ages, as white supremacy exerts itself not only over Black bodies, but over women's bodies too. False narratives rooted in antiquated religiosity and bigoted ideas from hundreds of years ago are used to justify this, and find willing audiences and believers.

In India, religious sectarianism and political authoritarianism go hand in hand, and violence grows as democracy dies. Once again, false narratives of Indian history are in play, narratives that privilege the majority and oppress minorities; and these narratives, let it be said, are popular, just as the Russian tyrant's lies are believed.

This, now, is the ugly dailiness of the world. How should we respond? It has been said, I have said it myself, that the powerful may own the present, but writers own the future, for it is through our work, or the best of it at least, the work which endures into that future, that the present misdeeds of the powerful will be judged. But how can we think of the future when the present screams for our attention, and what, if we turn away from posterity and pay attention to this dreadful moment, can we usefully or effectively do? A poem will not stop a bullet. A novel cannot defuse a bomb. Not all our satirists are heroes.

But we are not helpless. Even after Orpheus was torn to pieces, his severed head, floating down the river Hebrus, went on singing, reminding us that the song is stronger than death. We can sing the truth and name the liars, we can join in solidarity with our fellows on the front lines and magnify their voices by adding our own to them.

Above all, we must understand that stories are at the heart of what's happening, and the dishonest narratives of oppressors have proved attractive to many. So we must work to overturn the false narratives of tyrants, populists, and fools by telling better stories than they do, stories within which people want to live.

The battleground is not only on the battlefield. The stories we live in are contested territories too. Perhaps we can seek to emulate Joyce's Dedalus, who sought to forge, in the smithy of his soul, the uncreated conscience of his race. We can emulate Orpheus and sing on in the face of horror, and not stop singing until the tide turns, and a better day begins.

Revisiting this text almost eleven months later, eleven months during which my own life had been transformed by the violence unleashed by a false narrative, I understood that my second-chance life could not content itself with private pleasures alone. Love, above all things, and work, of course, but there was a war to fight on many fronts—against the bigoted revisionism that sought to rewrite history, whether in New Delhi or in Florida; against the cynical powers that sought to erase the two original sins of the United States, slavery and the oppression and geno-cide of the continent's original inhabitants; against fantasies of an idealized past (when exactly was America "great" in the way those red hats wanted to re-create?); against the self-harming lies that had taken Britain out of Europe. I could not sit idly by while these battles raged. In this struggle, too, I would—I had to—remain involved.

There was, however, one argument I was uninterested in tak-ing further: The argument that had bedeviled my life. The argu-ment about God.

I will express here, one last time, my view of religion—any religion, all religions—and then that, as far as I'm concerned, will be that. I don't believe in the "evidence of things not seen." I'm not religious. I come from a family of mostly not-religious people. (My youngest sister, Nabeelah, who died too soon, was an exception. She was devout.) I have never felt the need for religious faith to help me comprehend and deal with the world. However, I understand that for many people religion provides a moral anchor and seems essential. And in my view, the private faith of anyone is nobody's business except that of the individual concerned. I have no issue with religion when it occupies this private space and doesn't seek to impose its values on others. But when religion becomes politicized, even weaponized, then it's everybody's business, because of its capacity for harm.

I always remember that in the time of the French Enlightenment the enemy in the battle for freedom was not so much the State as the Church. The Catholic Church, with its arsenal of weapons—blasphemy, anathema, excommunication, as well as actual weapons of torture in the hands of the Inquisition—was in the business of placing its rigid limiting points on thought: *This far and no further.* And the writers and philosophers of the Enlightenment made it their business to challenge that authority and break those restrictions. Out of that struggle came the ideas Thomas Paine brought to America and which formed the basis of the essays *Common Sense* and *The American Crisis,* which inspired the independence movement, the Founding Fathers, and the modern concept of human rights.

In India, in the aftermath of the bloodbath of the Partition massacres that spread across the subcontinent at the time of independence from British rule and the creation of the states of India and Pakistan—Hindus massacred by Muslims, Muslims by Hindus, somewhere between one and two million people dead—another group of founding fathers, led by Mahatma Gandhi and Jawaharlal Nehru, resolved that the only way to ensure peace in India was to remove religion from the public sphere. The new Constitution of India was therefore wholly secular in language and intention, and that has endured until the present moment, when the current administration seeks to undermine those secular foundations, discredit those founders, and create an overtly religious, majoritarian Hindu state.

When the faithful believe that what they believe must be forced upon others who do not believe it, or when they believe that nonbelievers should be prevented from the robust or humorous expression of their nonbelief, then there's a problem. The weaponizing of Christianity in the United States has resulted in the overturning of *Roe v. Wade* and the ongoing battle over abortion, and women's right to choose. As I say above, the weaponizing of a kind of radical Hinduism by the current Indian leadership has led to much sectarian trouble, and even violence. And the weaponizing of Islam around the world has led directly to the terror reigns of the Taliban and the ayatollahs, to the stifling society of Saudi Arabia, to the knife attack against Naguib Mahfouz, to the assaults on free thought and the oppression of women in many Islamic states, and, to be personal, to the attack against me.

Many people, liberal as well as conservative, find themselves in difficulty when asked to criticize religion. But if we could simply make the distinction between private religious faith and public, politicized ideology, it would be easier to see things as they are and to speak out without worrying about offended sensibilities. In private life, believe what you will. But in the rough-and-tumble world of politics and public life, no ideas can be ring-fenced and protected against criticism.

All religions concern themselves with origin stories, accounts of the creation of the world by one or many supernatural beings. This is my origin story about religions themselves. I imagine that long ago, before our early ancestors had any scientific understanding of the universe, when they believed we lived under a dish, with the light of heaven shining through the holes in that dish, and other such tales, they reached for fabulist answers to the great existential questions—How did we get here? How did *here* get here?—and the concept of a sky god or gods, a Father-Creator or a pantheon of such beings, evolved. Then, as those ancestors sought to codify ideas of right and wrong, proper and improper behavior, as they asked the further great question, *Now that we are here, how shall we live?*, so the sky gods, the Valhalla gods, the Kailash gods began to be moral arbiters as well (although, in the pantheistic religions, the large array of deities contained many who didn't behave particularly well, who could not be said to be shining moral examples). I have long thought of this hypothetical past as something like the childhood of the human race, when those distant relatives of ours needed gods in the way that children need parents, to explain their own existence and to give them rules and boundaries within which to grow up. But the time comes when we must grow up—or ought to, because for many people that time still hasn't come. If I may quote Saint Paul in 1 Corinthians 13:11: "When I was a child, I spoke as a child, I understood as a child, I thought as a child; but when I became a man, I put away childish things." We no longer need the parentlike authority figure(s) of a Creator or Creators to explain the universe, or our own evolution into ourselves. And we—or, let me more modestly say, I—have no need of commandments, popes, or god-men of any sort to hand down my morals to me. I have my own ethical sense, thank you very much. God did not hand down morality to us. We created God to embody our moral instincts.

I have one more thing to say, which I haven't said before. Even though I have always been influenced by much Muslim thought and art (for example, the Hamzanama sequence of paintings made during the reign of the Mughal emperor Akbar; the *Mantiq ut-Tair* or *Conference of the Birds*, the mystic-epic poem by Fariduddin Attar that is something like an Islamic *Pilgrim's Progress;* and the liberal philosophy of the Spanish Arab thinker and Aristotelian scholar Averroës, or Ibn Rushd, after whom my father named our family), I have come to realize that in some ways I have been more influenced by the Christian world than I realized. For one thing, I love the music. Many of the hymns are forever stuck in my head, and to this day I can sing "O Come, All Ye Faithful," or "Adeste, Fideles," in Latin. I remember with pleasure the time the whole of my British boarding school, Rugby, took part in a rendition of Handel's *Messiah* in William Butterfield's red-brick Gothic Revival school chapel, and I lustily sang along in the "Hallelujah Chorus." I can't forget the beauty of the voices of the King's College choir, singing in the Cambridge chapel that I have always thought to be the most beautiful building in England, their melodies haunting the misty lawns and courtyards of my university home. And not only have I just quoted Paul in 1 Corinthians, I realize that I also quoted him, uncredited, earlier in this book, when I talked about seeing as through a glass darkly (which is, in fact, from 1 Corinthians 13:12). In fact the language of the King James Bible, or Authorized Version, often slips out of my mouth. Ever since I read P. G. Wodehouse's Jeeves and Bertie comic masterpiece *Joy in the Morning* I have been fond of Psalm 30 ("weeping may endure for a night, but joy cometh in the morning"). And what is one to do about Leonardo da Vinci, and Michelangelo, and all the rest of them? A couple of years ago, Eliza and I were in the Sistine Chapel, looking upward, while the guards intoned gravely, *"Silenzio, no foto."* Overwhelmed by beauty as I was, my rebellious atheist self managed to get quite a few photos.

So: yes, Christian art, architecture, music, even the Old Testament have made their way deep into my being, as well as their Muslim and Hindu counterparts. (*Victory City* is deeply influenced by Hindu narratives, as was *Midnight's Children* long ago.) None of which makes a believer of me. My godlessness remains intact. That isn't going to change in this second-chance life.

———

On January 7, 1938, in Paris, when almost all his major works, with the exception of *More Pricks Than Kicks*, remained unwritten, and when he was working on his novel *Murphy*, Samuel Beckett was walking down the Avenue de la Porte-d'Orléans on his way home from a movie when he was confronted by a pimp named Prudent, who wanted money from him. Beckett pushed Prudent away, whereupon the pimp pulled out a knife and stabbed the author in the chest, narrowly missing the left lung and the heart. Beckett was taken to the nearest hospital, l'Hôpital Broussais, bleeding heavily, and only just survived; James Joyce paid for the costs of a private room for him in the hospital.

As I was reading about this—another literary immortal, another knife attack—I began to scold myself. What was this, a club? Why was I trying to surround myself with the shades of these wounded giants? It was foolish. I should stop.

Then I read that after Beckett was released from the hospital he went to the pimp's trial, met Prudent in the courtroom, and asked him why he had done it. This was the pimp's reply: *"Je ne sais pas, monsieur. Je m'excuse."* I don't know, sir. I'm sorry. It wasn't much of an answer but when I read it, it made me want to look my assailant in the face, as Beckett had, and speak directly to him.

As far as I knew, the fellow was still pleading not guilty. If that didn't change, there would have to be a full-blown trial, and, my attorney, Nic, told me, I would probably have to go and give evidence in person.

"Do I have to actually be there?" I asked. "Could it be done remotely?"

"If I was the prosecuting attorney," Nic said, "I'd want you in court. To have the victim of the assault present would be very powerful."

That's fine, I thought. *I'm ready to do that.*

Nic said he would put in a call to the U.S. attorney's office to see how their work on the attempted-murder and aggravated-assault charges was progressing, and to the feds as well, to see where they were at with their effort to build a terrorism case. Yeah, I thought. If Samuel Beckett could confront his pimp in court, then I could damn well confront mine.

———

I had agreed to do one interview for every major translation of *Victory City*. These were Zoom interviews, with Eduardo Lago for *El País*, Maurizio Molinari for *La Repubblica*, Adam Soboczynski for *Die Zeit*. But then *Die Zeit* had the idea of inviting Eliza to make a portrait of me, which they would use with the interview. She was happy to agree. And on a Sunday in early April, the first really sunny day of spring, we went to Central Park, up near the reservoir, where the cherry blossom was everywhere. There were runners, walkers, musicians, people lounging on the grass, people lounging in rowboats; the city was out enjoying the beautiful day.

A camera draws attention, people want to see what it's pointing at, and so I was recognized by many people all afternoon. It was good to see how supportive, even celebratory, these recognitions were. New Yorkers are good at not intruding too much. They wave and then jog on, they smile broadly and then get on with their own lives, they make two-thumbs-up gestures, they call out happy, encouraging words. They don't stop. They don't bother you. They move on. I loved being there, in the park with my fellow citizens, all of us celebrating life in our own fashions. Eliza photographed me wreathed in blossom. The picture was a big hit, first in *Die Zeit*, and then—because it was picked up by other newspapers—elsewhere in Europe. It was an emotional photograph. There was love on both sides of the camera. It was a photograph of love.

Then it was our anniversary, May Day, six years since my encounter with the sliding glass door. Mayday, *m'aidez,* help me, the international distress signal. Eliza had come to my rescue on that roof terrace when we met. And then stayed, and changed my life for the better. And now was in the process of rescuing me again. We went to one of our favorite spots, a French place in Tribeca, and raised a glass.

———

Lawyer Nic (young, dynamic, smart, really good at his job) now thought it probable that the A. would change his plea to "guilty" and seek some sort of plea bargain.

Well, reality bites, I thought. Maybe he will finally understand that there were a thousand-plus witnesses to the crime.

"One thing's unusual," Nic said. "Usually when a federal case is introduced, the state case falls away. But it looks like there are two cases here, proceeding side by side, both the state case and a new federal case as well."

"And he might agree to plead guilty to both charges?"

"I'm sure his lawyers would want a global settlement. Both the cases together. There are things I have to clarify. But, big picture, the state charge we know, attempted murder and aggravated assault. It looks like the federal charge will be terrorism— providing material support to a known terrorist entity, or some language of that sort. He would plead guilty to all of it and be sentenced in both courts and serve the two sentences, one after the other."

"And how long might the sentences be?"

"I don't have any definite answer to give you. But, very approximately, if this were to happen, he would serve, in total, somewhere in the vicinity of thirty or forty years."

I thought: *Forty years from now I'll be one hundred and sixteen years old. So that's probably all right.*

I asked, "What about parole? What about time reduced for good behavior? This guy is very young. I don't want him walking the streets when he's forty-something, looking for me."

Nic said: "In the case of a federal sentence, there's no parole. He has to do the time. At the most he could get a fifteen-to-twenty-percent reduction because of good behavior. So, if he's sentenced to twenty, he'll do about seventeen for sure. And if he gets another twenty in the state court, that's probably another seventeen. It's hard to be exact, because the judge in each case has some leeway in the sentencing."

"I see. It's hard to feel pleased when it's so vague and we don't even know if he will change his plea. I just want to say, I've heard no word of regret or remorse from him, or through his lawyer, in eight months. That makes him a dangerous man, in my book."

"Understood."

"What happens if there is a plea bargain and I don't like the deal?"

"Well, you don't have a right of veto. You have the right as the victim to know what is being discussed, and what has been or will be agreed, and you absolutely have the right to express your opinion of that, as clearly as you want."

"So that would give us leverage."

"Maybe. Some."

"And where would all this happen? And when?"

"The state case would be tried in Chautauqua County Court. The federal case would be in Buffalo."

"Would they be roughly at the same time?"

"No. There would be a gap between the two. And in each case there would also be a gap between the guilty plea and the sentencing."

"How long?"

"It could all take many months. It might not be done before the middle of next year."

"Jesus, it's slow."

When I put down the phone I thought: *My Samuel Beckett moment could actually happen. That day could be about to arrive.*

The 2023 PEN Gala, at which I was to receive the Centenary Courage Award, was particularly meaningful to me. My association with PEN America had been long and deep. I was a past president and a co-founder of the PEN World Voices Festival, and we had been fighting the good fight together for decades. Unfortunately, sometimes the fight wasn't so good, and was just a brawl. I couldn't forget that eight years earlier, in April 2015, when this same Courage Award had been offered to the murdered cartoonists of the French satirical magazine *Charlie Hebdo,* an upsetting number of prominent writers objected because the magazine had occasionally lampooned Islam. It had poked fun at Roman Catholicism and at Israel far more often, and viciously satirized the French government, but it was characterized by these literary eminences as Islamophobic and statist, even though some of them admitted to never having seen a copy of *Charlie* and not being able to read French, anyway. It was a bitter quarrel. Friendships were broken, including several of mine, because I thought, and still think, that failing to stand by our colleagues who had been slaughtered by Islamist terrorists for drawing pictures was a morally confused thing to do. I couldn't help wondering what the anti-*Charlie* clique thought of the award to me. Perhaps they weren't in favor of that, either. I can't say. None of them has contacted me in several years. As far as I know, not a single one of them has commented on the attack against me, or on the PEN award.

All of that added a little background piquancy to the PEN event, but that wasn't where the focus of my attention was. The evening was joyful because I felt I was finally rejoining the world of writers, and finding myself once again among the closest thing I had to "my people." I was immensely happy to be there, in the Museum of Natural History, under the whale, with friends. It was another big step back into the world—the biggest so far.

In my speech at the Gala, I paid tribute to all those who had come to my rescue at Chautauqua. "I was the target that day, but they were the heroes." I talked about how important PEN was "at this moment when books and libraries as well as authors are so widely under siege." And I concluded my remarks in this way, using, somewhat to my surprise, an old Marxist slogan: "Terror must not terrorize us. Violence must not deter us. *La lutte continue.* The struggle goes on."

(No, Philip, I said silently to the great Mr. Roth. The struggle is not over. You can keep your Post-it note.)

———

The PEN Gala was a moment of high optimism, and we were in good spirits, but the news on our friends was not comforting. Martin had been cremated in Florida, and Isabel didn't know what she would do next. Hanif had regained some movement in his limbs but not in his hands. He was desperate to return to England, but the physical therapy place he wanted to go to had no room. Paul had failed a breathing test and so could not be operated on to remove the sections of infected lung. It felt almost indecent to be in a positive mood.

A few days later, I heard again that a plea bargain with the A. might be a possibility. And the hypothetical prison term of thirty or forty years was not unrealistic. But nothing was certain.

All there was to do was to wait.

8

Closure?

I waited. Spring lengthened into summer, and in the summer of 2023 it was as if the Earth itself was ablaze. Fires in Canada turned the New York sky orange and made the air dangerous to breathe. Climate records were broken in Las Vegas, and in the soaring heat of Death Valley, people began to die. I remembered the 1961 science-fiction film *The Day the Earth Caught Fire*, in which, thanks to the actions of human beings, the Earth fell out of its orbit and plunged toward the sun. Yesterday's B-movie, today's news headline. *Earth in uncharted waters*, the BBC announced, and there were reports that fish were boiling in the sea.

Waiting is thinking, and to think deeply is, very often, to change one's mind. My own anger faded. It felt trivial when set beside the anger of the planet. It was a year since the attack, and on this unlovely anniversary I understood that three things had happened that had helped me on my journey toward coming to terms with what had happened. The first was the passage of time. Time might not heal all wounds, but it deadened the pain, and the nightmares went away. The second was therapy. My sessions with my therapist, Dr. Justin Richardson, had helped me more than I am able to put into words. And the third was the writing of this book. These things did not give me "closure," whatever that was, if it was even possible to find such a thing, but they did mean that the assault weighed less heavily on me than before. And as a result I was no longer certain that I wanted, or needed, to confront and address the A. in open court. The "Samuel Beckett moment" no longer felt essential to me.

The law moved painfully slowly in any case. Weeks passed, and I still had no definite indication of when the matter might come before either the state or the federal court. Finally, I was told that there was a "Huntley hearing" scheduled in August. A Huntley hearing is held to determine whether the court is going to prohibit the prosecution from using select statements made by the accused at the time of his/her arrest during a trial. Perhaps in this case the A.'s lawyer, a public defender, wanted to suppress his (highly self-incriminating) interview with the *New York Post*? However, at the hearing, the lawyer chose not to call any witnesses or present any evidence on his client's behalf. Trooper Zachary Colbin, the officer who arrested the A., did testify. A local paper reported that the A. told Colbin that he had a bag by the stage. Colbin asked if there were any bombs in the bag, which the A. told him there weren't—only knives were inside. The bag was located and searched. It was confirmed that knives were the only weapons discovered. So he had brought a selection of knives with him? That was decidedly odd. Risky enough to bring one weapon into an auditorium. To bring several was even riskier. Was he not concerned about a bag search? And how many knives? Had he planned to use more than one? Or had he found it hard to choose which one to use? Had it been a spur-of-the-moment decision? Or a random, doesn't-matter-which-one choice? Did he think he might pass them out to the audience and invite them to join in? I had no answers to these questions. At any rate, no rulings in the accused's favor were made. The prosecutors said they were moving forward to a trial, which would now take place at an unspecified date in 2024.

I asked Nic: "Does this mean that there won't be a plea bargain after all, and instead there will be a full-scale trial, at which I'll have to testify?"

"Probably not," Nic surmised. "Mr. A. would most likely still accept the reality of his situation and enter guilty pleas in both courts."

Okay, I thought. Of course I would go and testify if required. But that now felt like a civic duty. It was no longer a way of satisfying a need.

Why had my mind changed? Why was the "Samuel Beckett moment" seeming less necessary than it had a short time ago? Surely, at the very least, there was a satisfying drama inherent in the idea of the victim of a murderous assault, me, confronting the man who had tried to kill him? Surely I could think of something worth saying to the failed murderer? Was not the sheer surrealism of the scene appealing at some level to the author of so many surrealist scenes? Might it not be good for me?

The answer was straightforward. The more steps I took back into "ordinary" or "real" life, the less taste I had for this "extraordinary," "unreal" episode. What I cared about now was *continuing*, writing the next chapter in the book of life. The attack felt like a large red ink blot spilled over an earlier page. It was ugly, but it didn't ruin the book. One could turn the page, and go on.

I decided that, if in the end I was obliged to go to court and testify, I would want to tell him something like this:

Here we stand: the man who failed to kill an unarmed seventy-five-year-old writer, and the now seventy-six-year-old writer he failed to kill. And, somewhat to my surprise, I find I have very little to say to you. Our lives touched each other for an instant and then separated. Mine has improved since that day, while yours has deteriorated. You made a bad gamble and lost. I was the one with the luck.

People who believed they knew you well have described you as a person who would never harm anybody. But they didn't know you as well as they thought they did. You are revealed here as a would-be assassin, and an incompetent one at that. You deceived those people about your true nature, but you will never deceive anyone again. Now you stand naked before the world.

Perhaps, in the incarcerated decades that stretch out before you, you will learn introspection, and come to understand that you did something wrong. But you know what? I don't care. This, I think, is what I have come to this courtroom to say to you. I don't care about you, or the ideology that you claim to represent, and which you represent so poorly. I have my life, and my work, and there are people who love me. I care about those things.

Your intrusion into my life was violent and damaging, but now my life has resumed, and it is a life filled with love. I don't know what will fill your imprisoned days, but I'm pretty sure it won't be love. And if I think of you at all in the future, it will be with a dismissive shrug. I don't forgive you. I don't *not* forgive you. You are simply irrelevant to me. And from now on, for the rest of your days, you will be irrelevant to everyone else. I'm glad I have my life, and not yours. And my life will go on.

———

I couldn't help but think about my lost eye. However calm I had begun to feel, I had not come to terms with it. When I spoke to

David Remnick for *The New Yorker*, I told him that this book
would not be written in the third person, as my earlier autobio-
graphical memoir, *Joseph Anton*, had been, because when somebody wounds you fifteen times it definitely feels very first-person.
That's an "I-story." And now, I told myself, it's also an "eye" story.
Other eye stories were showing up in my thoughts. I remembered E.T.A. Hoffmann's terrifying Sandman (quite different
from Neil Gaiman's Sandman-character, "Dream"), who flings
burning sand into people's faces and then steals their melting
eyes out of their heads. I understood, reading Hoffmann, that I
was not the only person for whom blindness was the worst thing
in the world.

In José Saramago's novel *Blindness*, an epidemic of sightless-
ness strikes an unnamed city, whereupon the social order dis-
integrates and collapses, and violence, starvation, disease, and
terror follow. When I read it years earlier, I had found it extraordinary but had been disappointed by the ending, in which the
mass blindness ends as suddenly and inexplicably as it began,
and everyone can see again. I had had a similar reservation about
the ending of another celebrated novel about mass infection, Al-
bert Camus's *The Plague*, in which the eponymous plague also
simply peters out. In my newly one-eyed condition, I found
these endings even less satisfactory than before. Those of us who
are blind, or, in my case, half-blind, know very well that blindness does not simply go away.

And there was Odin, who sacrificed one of his eyes to be given
permission, in return, to drink from the well whose waters
granted him divine wisdom and total understanding. And there
was the Cyclops Polyphemus, whom Odysseus blinded . . .

All these eye-stories I reread with new interest, hoping, I suppose, for consolation. They gave me very little. I had gained no
divine wisdom, and much as I loved Capri, the island of the Cy-

clops, it was hard to identify with a man-eating monocular giant. Even if we had the loss of an eye in common.

When I did find consolation, and even inspiration, it was not in fiction or myth but in a true story, about the Nawab of Pataudi and the game of cricket. All cricket fans—certainly all Indian followers of the game—will know that Mansoor Ali Khan, the nawab, or ruler, of the tiny princely state of Pataudi, known as "Tiger," or, to some in England, as "the Noob," was one of the great stars of the sport, a batsman of real flair, captain of India, and a figure of infinite glamour, married to one movie star, Sharmila Tagore, and father of two more movie stars, Saif and Soha Ali Khan. But a few months before his illustrious international sporting career began, when he was barely twenty years old, he had been involved in a car accident and had lost the sight of one eye. It was difficult to believe that a one-eyed batsman, even one of exceptional gifts, could face up to the bowling of such fearsome fast bowlers as Wes Hall and Charlie Griffith of the West Indies, who were the Indian team's next opponents. But he did play, and did well, and was appointed captain—at that time the youngest player ever to become captain of any cricketing nation—and so his glorious career began. I decided that the Tiger would be my role model. If he could face up to the ferocious speed of Hall and Griffith, I should be able to manage to pour water into a glass without spilling it, cross sidewalks without colliding with other pedestrians, and in general succeed at being functional as a one-eyed man in a two-eyed world.

———

Who am I? Am I the same person as I was on August 11, or am I now another? In some ways I am obviously altered. The August 11 self would never have chosen a sportsman as his role model, no matter how gifted. And it's also true that others seem to assume I am different now. Others ask me, how will what has happened affect your writing? One questioner likened me to Nietzsche—of all people!—because he had said, when he began to suffer from extreme shortsightedness, that his way of writing had changed. It was assumed that mine would change too, both aesthetically and also in the substance of my thought. When this was proposed to me I reacted strongly. I said: "I don't believe it has, or should, or will, impact my writing style in any way at all. The style, form, and language of any writing project, whether fiction or nonfiction, is determined by the requirements of that project, and can vary from book to book, from the baroque to the stripped-down . . . I don't see what an act of violence such as the one I experienced has to contribute to art." Saying this, I remembered something else I used to say in the life before August 11. I would tell people, "Imagine that you knew nothing about me, that you had arrived from another planet, perhaps, and had been given my books to read, and you had never heard my name or been told anything about my life or about the attack on *The Satanic Verses* in 1989. Then, if you read my books in chronological order, I don't believe you would find yourself thinking, *Something calamitous happened to this writer's life in 1989.* The books are on their own journey." I recalled thinking back then that there were two ways in which the fatwa could derail me, destroy me as an artist: if I started writing "frightened" books, or if I started writing "revenge" books. Both options would destroy my individuality and independence and make me no more than a creature of that attack. It would own me, and I would no longer be myself. So the only true way, the only way to survive as an artist, was to understand the literary path I was on, to accept the journey I had chosen, and to continue to go down that path. That had required an act of will. And now I was being asked the question again. Who was I? And could I remain myself?

Many writers have been aware of a divide between their pub-

lic and private selves. Long ago, in Berlin, I was having a coffee
with Günter Grass at a café on Unter den Linden and he said,
"Sometimes I feel that there are two people, Günter and Grass.
Günter is the husband of my wife, the father of my children, the
friend of my friends, and lives at my home. Grass is somewhere
out there in the world, making noise, making trouble." Then
there is the famous text by Jorge Luis Borges "Borges and I," in
which he says: "The other one, the one called Borges, is the one
things happen to. . . . I shall remain in Borges, not in myself (if it
is true that I am someone), but I recognize myself less in his
books than in many others or in the laborious strumming of a
guitar. . . . I do not know which of us has written this page." And
in an extreme but related case, Graham Greene discovered that
he had an alter ego, a false self moving through a social milieu
not unlike his own, claiming to be the real Greene. He would
receive messages from unknown women recounting their romantic encounters, and see newspaper photographs of the other
Greene in places he hadn't visited when the pictures were taken.
Once, in Chile, he was accused of being the fake Graham Greene
himself. They never met, the real one and the other, but, the
story goes, Greene once arrived at a hotel to check in and discovered that the other Graham Greene had just checked out.

Ever since 1989, I have felt uneasy about the other Rushdies
circulating in the world. I too am both "Salman" and "Rushdie."
There is the demon Rushdie invented by, I have to say, many
Muslims—this is the Rushdie the A. believed he wanted to kill.
There is the arrogant, egotistical Rushdie created by the British
tabloids back in the day (this one appears presently to be taking
a back seat). There is party-animal Rushdie. And now, post–
August 12, there is the more sympathetically imagined "good
Rushdie," the near-martyr, the free-speech icon, but even this
one has things in common with all the "bad Rushdies": it has

very little to do with the Salman sitting at home, the husband of his wife, the father of his sons, the friend of his friends, trying to get over what happened to him, still trying to write his books. And they all distract attention from the books themselves. In some way they all make it *unnecessary* to read the books. And that, to my mind, is the greatest damage I've suffered, both before August 12 and because of August 12. I've become a strange fish, famous not so much for my books as for the mishaps of my life. So the correct answer to the question "How will this affect your writing?" is: It will affect the way my writing is read. Or not read. Or both.

However, I need to accept that I am both "Salman" and "Rushdie"—to retain the optimism needed for the creating of fictions, and the hope that my novels will continue to find readers (assuming I can go on finding the novels), and to add to that the willingness to go on fighting the good fight. If fortune has turned me into a sort of virtuous liberty-loving Barbie doll, Free-Expression Rushdie, then I will embrace that fate. Maybe this is what "closure" means for me: an acceptance of reality, and forward movement through that reality.

———

In the immediate aftermath of the *Charlie Hebdo* murders, I wrote this: "Religion, an ancient form of unreason, when combined with modern weaponry becomes a real threat to our freedoms. Religious totalitarianism has caused a deadly mutation in the heart of Islam and we see the tragic consequences in Paris today. I stand with *Charlie Hebdo*, as we all must, to defend the art of satire, which has always been a force for liberty and against tyranny, dishonesty and stupidity. 'Respect for religion' has become a code phrase meaning 'fear of religion.' Religions, like all other ideas, deserve criticism, satire, and, yes, our fearless disrespect." In the case of the A.'s attack on me, I would substitute the word "technology" for "weaponry," because there's nothing modern about a knife, and yet he, the A., is wholly a product of the new technologies of our information age, for which "disinformation age" might be a more accurate name. The groupthink-manufacturing giants, YouTube, Facebook, Twitter, and violent video games were his teachers. Added to what appeared to be a malleable personality which found in the groupthink of radical Islam a structure for the identity it needed, they produced a self that almost became a murderer.

John Locke wrote, "I have always thought the actions of men the best interpreters of their thoughts." The knife attack told us all we needed to know about the A.'s interior life. The trial would happen when it happened, I would testify if required to do so, and the sentence would be whatever it would be. It no longer felt as important as it had.

———

Thirteen months after the attack, I went back to Chautauqua. I had decided it was something I needed to do for myself: to return to the scene of the crime, and feel myself standing up again, healthy and strong—or at least relatively healthy and no longer weak—in the place where I had fallen down and very nearly died; where Death had aimed at me, and (narrowly) missed. I hoped it would feel like a rite of overcoming, and help me to leave that terrible day behind.

"I'm going with you," Eliza said. "This time I'm not letting you make that trip alone."

As the day of the journey approached, the prospect began occasionally to weigh on me. My mind circled back to that earlier day, and big emotions I thought I'd dealt with welled up again. Then, at other times, it felt much less powerful. It was possible,

I thought, that I would react to being at the amphitheater again with little more than a shrug: *Yeah, that happened, but that was then and this is now. Nothing to see here. Let's move along.* I asked Eliza if the approaching visit was making her feel weird. "Of course it is," she said. "It's natural that it would be." I told her I really didn't know how being back there would affect me— deeply, or hardly at all, or somewhere in between. "My moods swing," I said. Maybe that was natural, too.

"We can't know," she said. "We can only go and find out."

I had spoken to Shannon Rozner, a senior vice-president at the Institution, about my wish to visit, and she was understanding and helpful. The earliest date that worked for everyone was, strangely, September 11, the twenty-second anniversary of another, much bigger, world-changing terrorist attack. My own story was and is very small when set beside that horror. But it's also a part of the same story, the story of religious-terrorist violence. 9/11 taught us that an aircraft could be a knife, too. Those planes, American Airlines Flight 11 and United Airlines Flight 175, slashed like deadly blades into the bodies of their targets, the Twin Towers, and thousands of human beings inside those murdered giants were less lucky than I.

I remembered a *Doonesbury* comic strip in which one character tells another: "You know, I really miss September 10th." That sentence, speaking so tenderly as it did of lost innocence, even a lost world, had stayed with me, and now I found myself thinking, "You know, I really miss August 11." I wanted very badly to be, once again, that carefree fellow looking up at the full moon over the lake, a writer with a new novel soon to be published, and a man in love. Was that what this return journey might conjure up? Not "closure," but a deepened longing for an irretrievably lost past, that past from which the knife had cut me away, leaving an ache for which there was no cure? Maybe I was going to Chautauqua to face up to the unbearable knowledge, common to all human beings, that it would never be yesterday again.

We can't know. We can only go and find out.

At 5 A.M. on September 11, our flight was canceled. Eliza and I had both been thinking deeply about the visit to prepare for it, and this was an emotional blow. But we had been dealt far worse blows in the past year and survived. We rearranged the trip for a week later, and for some reason the new date felt less stressful to both of us than the original one.

Shortly before we left, I learned that the A. had rejected the plea deal, perplexing everyone. So the two trials, state and federal, would in all probability have to take place. Maybe he was not thinking rationally, because it was still the case that over a thousand people had seen him doing the thing he claimed to be not guilty of having done. Maybe he would offer an insanity defense? Or maybe he wanted a couple of days' grandstanding in court, playing the radical hero to an audience far away. Maybe he would change his mind again. *Do whatever you want,* I thought. *You go your way and I'll go mine.*

———

Monday, September 18, was one year, one month, and one week since my last journey to Chautauqua. Both of us woke up feeling very calm and "normal." I was more worried about Eliza than myself. She had never been to Chautauqua, so she would be seeing the amphitheater for the first time, and I knew that would arouse strong feelings in her. But she insisted that it was a very good idea to go. "I'll be okay," she told me. "And actually, I'm more worried about you."

On the flight it occurred to me to find out where the Chautauqua County Jail, where the A. was being held in custody, might be located. If it wasn't too far from our destination, the Chautauqua Institution, I thought, I'd like to go and stand in front of it, just to have that picture in my mind's eye. I learned that it was only a short drive between the two locations, less than ten minutes. "Let's do it," I said to Eliza. She was briefly hesitant, but then agreed.

The weather that day was strangely auspicious. In the morning in New York City it was raining heavily, but when we reached Buffalo, and for the rest of our visit, there was bright sunshine; it had become a beautiful day, just as it had been on August 11 and 12 a year earlier. It was as if the universe had decided to re-create the conditions of my previous visit for our benefit. That was helpful. If it had been a stormy, rainy day at Chautauqua, our experience would have been different: darker, more ominous, less relaxed. But we had blue skies to greet us and keep our spirits light. (Later, when we were on the road back to the airport, the clouds closed in and the downpour began again. It felt theatrical—the curtain of the day had gone up for us on our arrival, and then come down again as we left.)

We passed through idyllic small towns and villages, their delightful aspect marred only by a few TRUMP signs. Place names moved past us. Seneca, on the original land of the Seneca people, who were part of the Iroquois Confederacy. Angola, so named in the nineteenth century because the population had supported missionary activity in Africa. Eden, "the Garden Spot." Dunkirk, which had taken its name from Dunkerque in France long before World War II. And my favorite, Fredonia. As any film buff could tell you, *Freed*onia is the name of the imaginary country of which Groucho Marx becomes leader in the Marx Brothers' 1933 classic, *Duck Soup*. Snatches of dialogue from the movie came back to me and put a smile on my face. It felt good to have some foolishness in my head for a moment.

Why, a four-year-old child could understand this report. Run out and find me a four-year-old child. I can't make head or tail out of it.

But then another name approached us on a road sign. *Erie. 20 miles after the PA line*. That evoked strong memories of the Hamot hospital and put a somber complexion on the morning.

Eliza didn't tell me until much later—when we were back home in New York City—that on the plane she had been assailed by painful flashback memories of her flight to Erie on the day of the attack with awful words echoing in her ears. *He's not going to make it*. She had forced herself to turn her thoughts away from that memory to focus on this day, and what it might mean for us both.

———

The jail was a small set of unimposing red-brick buildings. To the left was the police block. The cell block was on the right, behind barbed wire. I took a photograph of it and sent it to Sameen, who texted back, "It looks so ordinary." Yes, it did. But it had an unexpected effect on me. As I stood looking at it, trying to picture the A. in his black-and-white prison uniform somewhere in there, I felt foolishly happy and wanted, absurdly, to dance. "Stop it," Eliza warned me. "I want to take a picture of you in front of this place, and you shouldn't be grinning or hopping about." We didn't stay long. We didn't need to. But I was glad to have seen the place where my would-be murderer, I hoped and expected, might spend a substantial portion of his life.

———

In the sunlight, the Chautauqua Institution looked at its best. It was very quiet. The season was over, and the ten thousand or so people who came here for the summer program of events had gone now, leaving behind only about four hundred year-round residents. Lake Chautauqua glistened in the background and the trees were still green, though here and there touched with gold. I could see the spot where I had stood at night and taken a picture of the full moon.

We were greeted by Shannon Rozner and Michael Hill, the president of the Institution. I understood at once that for them, as for us, this was a powerfully emotional moment.

"I have thought about you every single day since it happened," Michael said, and his voice broke as he added, "I'm so, so sorry."

"I'm glad to be back more or less in one piece," I said.

"It's so beautiful here," Eliza said.

"I've thought a lot about the dissonance between the beauty and peacefulness of the place and the ugly violence of the event," I said. "Somehow the gorgeousness of the setting makes the crime even more shocking."

"Exactly," Michael said. "And I'm so glad to see you looking so well. We all are."

Then it was time. We entered the amphitheater by the same stage door I had used a year earlier, and paused in the backstage area, where I had met Henry Reese's mother and been given my check, the bloodstained check that was now in prosecutorial hands as evidence. I could see that Eliza had become very emotional. So was I. But here we were, to do what we had come to do. Doors were opened and we went out onto the stage and stared out at the empty rows of seats, and they stared back at us.

The stage was empty too, a large expanse of polished wooden boards. I tried to re-create the moment for Eliza. There were two chairs, for Henry and me, I told her, approximately *here* and *here*, and the standing microphone from which Sony Ton-Aime had introduced us was over *there*. And the A.—when I first saw him—must have jumped up from a seat about halfway up on the right. *There.* And he ran fast and came up these steps. *Here.* And then the attack. And when I fell it was just about *here.* Right *here.*

I was doing what I had imagined and needed to do: standing up on the spot—on what I told myself was the exact spot—where I had fallen down. I felt, I confess, just a little bit triumphant as I stood there. I remembered, but refrained from reciting, lines from "Invictus" by W. E. Henley. "Under the bludgeonings of chance / My head is bloody, but unbowed."

After that, I told Eliza, they brought me back *here,* and then, after I don't know how long, there was the gurney to the helicopter, which had landed somewhere over *there.*

Michael said, "We brought the ambulance right to the back door, and this is the door through which he was taken out."

The Chautauqua folks very kindly left us alone in that enormous space, and for a long while all we wanted to do was embrace. We stood there and held each other tightly and told each other, *It's okay. It's good that we came. We're together. I love you. I love you too. This was important to do.*

I could see that it was hard for Eliza to be there, but also good, she said, that now she knew how it had been, how it had all looked; she didn't have to imagine it anymore. When they told her, "This is the door through which he was taken out," it was hard for her to bear, but she held it together. We held it together. I was very glad she was there. We hugged each other, telling each other wordlessly that we were there for each other, that we had come through the nightmare and it was okay. It would have been completely different—sadder, less of an affirmation, less restorative—if I had been there alone.

As for myself, it took me a while to understand what was happening to me. At first I was distracted from my own feelings by setting the scene for Eliza, and worrying about her well-being.

But as we stood there in the stillness I realized that a burden had lifted from me somehow, and the best word I could find for what I was feeling was *lightness*. A circle had been closed, and I was doing what I had hoped I could do here—I was making my peace with what had happened, making my peace with my life. I stood where I had almost been killed, wearing, I have to tell you, my *new* Ralph Lauren suit, and I felt . . . whole.

"I could see that this was good for you," Eliza said, "and that made it good for me too."

I remembered the question I had asked myself after the attack: Could our happiness survive such a blow? Standing there, on the stage of the Chautauqua amphitheater, I knew the answer. Yes, we had reconstructed our happiness, even if imperfectly. Even on this blue-sky day, I knew it was not the cloudless thing we had known before. It was a wounded happiness, and there was, and perhaps always would be, a shadow in the corner of it. But it was a strong happiness nevertheless, and as we embraced, I knew it would be enough.

"We're done here," I said to Eliza, taking her hand. "Let's go home."

ABOUT THE AUTHOR

SALMAN RUSHDIE is one of the world's most acclaimed, award-winning contemporary authors. Translated into over forty languages, his sixteen works of fiction include *Midnight's Children* – for which he won the Booker Prize in 1981, the Booker of Bookers on the 25th anniversary of the prize and Best of the Booker on the 40th anniversary – *Shame, The Ground Beneath Her Feet, The Satanic Verses, Haroun and the Sea of Stories* and *Quichotte* (shortlisted for the Booker Prize in 2019). In June 2007 he received a knighthood in the Queen's Birthday Honours and he joined the prestigious Companions of Honour in the Queen's Birthday Honours list in her Platinum Jubilee year. His international awards include the PEN/ Allen Foundation Literary Service Award, the National Arts Award, the French Prix du Meilleur Livre Étranger, the European Union's Aristeion Prize for Literature, the Budapest Grand Prize for Literature and the Italian Premio Grinzane Cavour. He is a member of the American Academy of Arts and Letters and a fellow of the American Academy of Arts and Sciences, and he is a Distinguished Writer in Residence at New York University. He is a former president of PEN America.

salmanrushdie.com
Facebook.com/salmanrushdieauthor
X: @SalmanRushdie